6 08

AL-ANON INLAND EMPIRE SERVICE CENTER
1012 E. COOLEY DR. STE. J-2
COLTON, CA 92324
PH. (714) 824-1516

D0058170

Second Edition

Al-Anon Family Group Headquarters, Inc.

New York   1986

© Al-Anon Family Group Headquarters Inc. 1965, 1971, 1973, 1977, 1984
P.O. Box 862, Midtown Station
New York, New York 10018-0862

Library of Congress Card No. 84-70190
ISBN 0-910034-55-9

Second Edition
Third Printing, May 1986

Approved by
World Service Conference
Al-Anon Family Groups

PRINTED IN THE UNITED STATES OF AMERICA

Other books about Al-Anon Family Groups:

      AL-ANON FAMILY GROUPS
        (formerly LIVING WITH AN ALCOHOLIC)
      THE DILEMMA OF THE ALCOHOLIC MARRIAGE
      ONE DAY AT A TIME IN AL-ANON
      FORUM FAVORITES
      ALATEEN—HOPE FOR CHILDREN OF ALCOHOLICS
      LOIS REMEMBERS
      AL-ANON'S TWELVE STEPS AND TWELVE TRADITIONS
      ALATEEN—A DAY AT A TIME
      AS WE UNDERSTOOD…
      FIRST STEPS: AL-ANON 35 YEARS OF BEGINNINGS

CONTENTS

THOSE WHO LIVE WITH THE PROBLEM

Contents

PREFACE

The Al-Anon fellowship has grown in public recognition and shared experience since the first edition of *AL-ANON FACES ALCOHOLISM* was published nearly twenty years ago. Today, Al-Anon, which includes Alateen, is a worldwide organization with a membership of some half million men, women and young people. This program provides an accessible community resource helping anyone who is deeply affected by the family disease of alcoholism. The second edition of *AL-ANON FACES ALCOHOLISM* looks at the Al-Anon program from three different perspectives.

First, Al-Anon is viewed through the eyes of professionals most closely associated with the recognition and treatment of alcoholism—doctors, psychologists, counselors, to name a few. Knowledge and understanding of the disease of alcoholism is an expanding field. Articles submitted by these leading practitioners have brought together all that is currently known of this disease. Al-Anon, in keeping with its Traditions, makes no attempt to recommend and endorse professional viewpoints. Professional contributors have described why and how they refer to Al-Anon. They have also expressed their opinions on the value of the Al-Anon program.

The personal stories of Al-Anon members that make up the second section have been expanded from the first edition. The diversity in background of these contributors demonstrates the growth of Al-Anon. Unfortunately, covering the complete range of experiences before Al-Anon is too broad for the scope of this book. But the unique nature of the program is demonstrated through each story—without exception each person found help in Al-Anon. A variety of experiences led to a common solution. It is this recognition that continues to draw the membership together into a close, spiritual fellowship.

The final section of the book is a short discussion of what the Al-Anon program is. Membership is open to anyone affected by problem drinking in a family member or a friend. It is a program for those who want it, not those who need it. Al-Anon means different things to different people. At meetings or through the Al-Anon literature, a gathering of past experience and collected wisdom is shared. Participation can lead to a new way of life for each individual member.

One of the Al-Anon Traditions is to pass on such knowledge to others. We hope that this book will help to do just that. It has been written for all interested people, but especially for anyone personally in need of help.

UNDERSTANDING ALCOHOLISM

The American Medical Association recognizes alcoholism as a disease which can be arrested but not cured. One of the symptoms is an uncontrollable desire to drink. An alcoholic is someone whose drinking causes a continuing, or growing, problem in any aspect of his or her life. If the alcoholic continues to drink, the compulsion to drink will get worse. The only method of arresting alcoholism is total abstinence. Most authorities agree that, even after years of sobriety, alcoholics can never again control their drinking.

All kinds of people are alcoholics. Most have families, friends and jobs. They function fairly well. But their drinking affects some part of their life, whether socially, in the workplace or within the family. Often all three areas are affected to some extent,

There are many successful treatments for alcoholism today. Alcoholics Anonymous is the most well-known and is widely regarded as the most effective. It is the nature of this disease that its victims do not believe they are ill. Therefore, hope for recovery lies in their ability to recognize the need for help, their desire to stop drinking, and their willingness to enter a program of recovery, such as Alcoholics Anonymous.

Those Who Work
With the Problem

In keeping with Al-Anon's Traditions, we neither endorse nor oppose the opinions, therapies or techniques shared here by professionals who work in the field of alcoholism. Rather, we acknowledge our gratitude for their willingness to share those opinions with us in this work.

ALCOHOLISM AND THE FAMILY

by Joan K. Jackson, Ph.D.

It is no longer possible to consider alcoholism as a disease affecting only the alcoholic. Others in the family react to the illness. There is considerable evidence that it had disturbing effects on the personalities of family members, and family studies indicate that a minimum of one other relative is directly involved.

The relationship between the alcoholic and the family is not a one-way relationship. The family also affects the alcoholic and his or her illness. (The very existence of family ties is related to recovery from alcoholism.) Some families are successful in helping the alcoholic member to recognize a need for help and to support treatment efforts. Others may discourage the alcoholic from seeking treatment and may actually encourage persistence of the illness. It is now believed that *the most successful treatment of alcoholism involves helping both the alcoholic and those members of the family who are directly involved in the alcoholic's behavior.*

The Impact of Alcoholism on the Family

When two or more persons live together over a period of time, patterns of relating to one another evolve. In a family a division of functions occurs and roles interlock. For the family to function smoothly, each person must play an appropriate role in a predictable manner. When the family as a whole is functioning smoothly, individual members also tend to function well. Everyone is aware of where he or she fits in, of what is expected, and of what in turn, can be expected from others. When this organization is disrupted, repercussions are felt by each family member and a crisis is underway.

Family crises often follow a similar pattern, regardless of what may have precipitated them. Frequently there is an initial denial that a problem exists. The family tries to continue its usual behavior patterns until it is obvious that these patterns are no longer effective. At this point there is a downward slump in organization. Roles are played with less enthusiasm, and there is an increase in tensions and strained relationships. Finally an improvement may occur as some adjustive technique is successful. Family organization then becomes stabilized at a new level. At each phase of the crisis there is a reshuffling of roles among family members, changes in status and prestige, changes in "self" and "other" images, shifts in family solidarity and self-sufficiency and in visibility of the crisis to outsiders. While the crisis is in process, considerable mental conflict is engendered in all family members, and personality distortion occurs. The phases vary in length and intensity, depending on the nature of the crisis and the nature of the individuals involved in it.

When one of the adults in a family becomes an alcoholic, there are usually recurrent, subsidiary crises that complicate the overall situation and attempts at resolving it. Shame, unemployment, impoverishment, desertion and return, non-support, infidelity, violence, imprisonment, illness and progressive dissension may also occur.

For most types of family crisis there are cultural prescriptions for what to do to end the crisis. In the case of alcoholism, however, despite some lessening of the social stigma, our culture still takes the position that this problem is shameful and should not occur. Thus, when facing alcoholism, the family is in a social situation that is largely unstructured, so it must find the techniques for handling the crisis through trial and error and without social support. In many respects there are marked similarities between the type of family crisis brought about by alcoholism and those precipitated by mental illness.

Attempts to Deny the Problem

Full-blown alcoholism is rarely a sudden event. It is usually heralded by widely-spaced incidents of excessive drinking, each of which sets off a small family crisis. Both husband and wife try to find reasons for the episode, hoping to avoid the family situations that appear to have caused the drinking. In their search for explanations, they may try to define the situation as controllable, understandable and "perfectly normal." Between drinking episodes both may feel guilty about their behavior and about their impact on each other. Gradually not only the drinking problem but also the other problems in the marriage are denied or side-stepped.

It takes some time before the non-alcoholic spouse realizes that the drinking is neither normal nor controllable behavior. It takes the alcoholic considerably longer to come to the same conclusion. The cultural view that alcoholics are skid row bums and/or are constantly inebriated also serves to keep the situation clouded. Friends compound the confusion. If the spouse compares his or her situation with them, some show parallels in

behavior and others are in marked contrast. If the spouse con-
sults friends, they tend to discount his or her concerns, making
it easier to deny that a problem exists and adding to mounting
guilt.

During this stage social isolation of the family often begins.
To a certain degree others withdraw after one or more episodes
of inappropriate behavior by the alcoholic. For the most part,
however, the isolation is brought about by the family withdraw-
ing *itself* socially. Members fear the reaction of others to the increasingly unpredictable public behavior of the alcoholic; they
fear that their own inability to cope effectively with such
episodes will be obvious to outsiders; they fear that others will
come to know the full extent of the drinking. To protect
themselves from their distress and from what they see as inevitable social exclusion, the family cuts down on social activities and withdraws into the home.

Attempts to Eliminate the Problem

The next stage begins when the family defines the alcoholic's
drinking behavior as "not normal." Frantic efforts are now
made to eliminate the problem. Lacking clear-cut cultural
prescriptions for a solution to this situation, such efforts must
be trial-and-error in nature. In rapid succession, the wife
threatens to leave the husband, babies him during his
hangovers, drinks with him, hides or empties his bottles, cur-
tails money, tries to understand his problem, keeps his liquor
handy for him, and nags at him. Similar sequences of events occur when a husband attempts to deal with an alcoholic wife. In
any case, efforts to change the situation fail. Gradually the
family becomes so preoccupied with the problem of discovering

how to keep the alcoholic sober that long-term goals recede into the background.

At this time, isolation for the family reaches its peak. This isolation magnifies the importance of all intrafamily interactions and events. Almost all thought becomes drinking-centered. Drinking comes to symbolize all conflicts between the husband and wife, and even parent-child conflicts are regarded as indirect derivatives of the drinking behavior. Attempts increase to keep the social visibility of the drinking at the lowest possible level.

The husband-wife alienation also accelerates. Each feels resentful of the other. Each feels misunderstood and unable to understand. Both search frantically for the reasons for the drinking, believing that if the reason could be discovered, all family members could gear their behavior in a way to make the drinking unnecessary.

The wife feels increasingly inadequate as a wife, mother, woman and person. She may feel she has failed to make a happy and united home for her husband and children. The husband's frequent comments to the effect that *her* behavior causes his drinking, and her own concern that this may be true, intensifies the process of self-devaluation. The non-alcoholic husband also feels inadequate as a marital partner, frequently feeling lonely and abandoned by his spouse. He may experience great concern about the deterioration of the household and increasing anxiety as to the effects of his wife's alcoholism on their children. He, too, is plagued by feelings of guilt and helplessness.

Disorganization

A fitting title for this stage could be *"What's the Use?"* Nothing seems effective in stabilizing the alcoholic. Efforts to change the situation become, at best, sporadic. Behavior is geared to relieve tensions rather than to achieve goals. The family gives up trying to understand the alcoholic. They do not care if the neighbors know about the drinking. The children may be told their father or mother is a drunk. They are no longer required to show that parent affection or respect. When the alcoholic parent is male, the myth that the father still has an important status in the family is dropped when he no longer supports them, is imprisoned, is caught in infidelity or disappears for long periods of time. The family ceases to care about its self-sufficiency and may begin to resort to public agencies for financial and other help, often feeling a loss of self-respect as a result.

The non-alcoholic partner becomes much concerned about his or her sanity. Such individuals find themselves engaging in tension-relieving behavior that is clearly goalless. They are aware of feeling tense, anxious and hostile. They come to think of the pre-crisis self as "the real me" and become frightened at how much they have changed.

Attempts to Reorganize in Spite of the Problem

The disorganized state usually ends when some alcohol-related crisis, which may be serious or may simply represent the straw that broke the camel's back, forces the family to take organized action. In some families this action takes the form of a physical separation from the alcoholic. In others, where such a step is felt to be too extreme, there is an effort to restructure the family along new lines of authority. When reorganization is thus attempted, this new phase has as its distinguishing characteristic the spouse who takes over. The alcoholic is ignored or is assigned the status of a recalcitrant child. When the non-drinking spouse's obligations to the alcoholic conflict with those toward the children, the decisions favor the children. Family ranks are closed progressively and the drinker is excluded.

As a result of the changed family organization, the alcoholic's behavior constitutes less of a problem. Hostility diminishes as the family no longer expects a change. Feelings of pity, exasperation and protectiveness may arise.

This reorganization has a stabilizing effect on the children. They find their environment and their non-alcoholic parent more consistent. Their relationships are more clearly defined. Guilt and anxiety diminish as they come to accept the non-drinker's view that the cause of the problem-drinking is not connected with the behavior of family members.

Long-term family goals and planning may begin again. If she has not done so already, the wife may take a job. If she does, she alleviates several problems. The family manages financially without the alcoholic; the wife becomes less socially isolated and is able to begin to regain a sense of competence. If necessary, help from public agencies is accepted and no longer impairs family self-respect. By taking over, the wife gradually regains her sense of worth. Her concerns about her emotional health decrease.

The husband of an alcoholic wife may start to cope with household and family problems by making arrangements for child care, by hiring household help, by taking part in increased activities with his children outside the home.

Despite such stabilization, however, subsidiary crises multiply. The alcoholic is violent or withdraws more often. Unemployment, legal problems and hospitalizations occur more frequently. Each crisis is temporarily disruptive to the new family organization. The recognition of these events as being caused by alcoholism, however, prevents a complete family breakdown.

The most serious type of crisis occurs if the alcoholic recognizes that he or she has a drinking problem and makes an effort to get help. Hope is mobilized. The family attempts to open its ranks in order to give the alcoholic the maximum chance for recovery. Roles are partially reshuffled and attempts are made at attitude change, only to be disrupted again if treatment is unsuccessful.

Efforts to Escape the Problem

Many husbands and some wives find it necessary to leave their alcoholic spouses outright. The problems involved in separating from the alcoholic are similar to problems involved in separation for other reasons. Some, however, are more difficult. The wife who could count on some financial support from her husband in earlier stages of alcoholism can no longer be sure of such assistance. The husband finds himself without emotional support. The mental conflict about deserting a sick person must be resolved, as well as painful feelings of responsibility for the alcoholism. The family that has experienced violence from the alcoholic may fear that separation will intensify the violence. When the decision is made to live apart because of the drinking, the alcoholic often gives up drinking for a while, thereby removing, at least temporarily, what is apparently the major reason for separation—and creating, in the process, much confusion and guilt in the non-alcoholic partner.

Other events, however, may have made separation more acceptable. The non-alcoholic spouse may have learned that the family can run smoothly without the alcoholic. Taking over control has bolstered the spouse's self-confidence. The family's orientation has shifted from inaction to action.

Reorganization of the Family

When recovery is actually underway, the family enters a difficult period of adjustment and reorganization. After many years of living in an alcoholic situation, a husband and wife now beginning a sober marriage may find their expectations of each other to be unrealistic and idealistic. Many problems arise if either spouse has managed the family alone for a considerable time. When the alcoholic wishes to be reinstated as a parent or as a full marital partner, difficulties inevitably follow. For example, the children are often unable to accept the alcoholic's resumption of the parental role. One parent has been mother and father to them for so long that it takes time to get used to consulting the other. Often the alcoholic parent tries to manage this change overnight, and the very pressure put on the children leads to defeat.

The spouse has difficulty believing that the change is permanent, and is often unwilling to relinquish control of family affairs even though this may be necessary to another's sobriety. Past failures to handle responsibility were a disaster for the family. Accustomed to avoiding issues that might upset the alcoholic, the spouse has difficulty discussing problems openly.

If managing roles are resumed, the spouse often feels resentful of the alcoholic's intrusion into territory once regarded as one's own. If detrimental decisions are made, the former feeling of superiority may be activated and may affect the relationship.

Gradually the difficulties related to alcoholism recede into the past, and family adjustment at some level is achieved. Problems about drinking may show up occasionally—perhaps when the time comes for a decision about permitting the children to drink, or when there are social pressures to drink.

Therapy and the Family

The major goal of the families of most alcoholics is to find some way of bringing about a change in the drinking. Often this involves getting the alcoholic into a treatment program. It is not at all unusual for family members to have mixed feelings toward the treatment agency. Hope that the alcoholic may recover is rekindled, and if sobriety ensues for any length of time, they are grateful. At the same time, they often feel resentment that an outside agency can accomplish what they have tried to do for years. They also resent the emotional support the alcoholic receives from the treatment agency, while they are left to cope with still another change in their relationship to him or her without such emotional support.

It is fortunate that in recent years most treatment programs for alcoholics have come to see the importance of involving family members. Most often it is the spouse who is included in the alcoholic's treatment, but sometimes children are also asked to take part. Joint treatment aims at getting a better understanding of the underlying emotional disturbances, the relationship between the alcoholic and the people who most frequently interact with the drinking behavior, and the treatment process. Joint treatment of the alcoholic and his family also has other advantages. Joint therapy emphasizes the marriage. With both partners coming for help, there is less likelihood that undertaking treatment will be construed as an admission of guilt or that therapy will be used as a weapon by one against the other. The non-alcoholic's entrance into therapy is an unspoken admission that that person also needs to change. It represents a hopeful attitude on the part of both the alcoholic and the partner that recovery is possible, which helps them to work things out together as a family unit.

A very important resource for the families of alcoholics is the Al-Anon Family Group program. While Al-Anon is similar in many important ways to other programs which help or include the families of alcoholics, it has some very significant differences. Unlike most programs, Al-Anon does not require that the alcoholic be undergoing treatment. It helps the families of recovering alcoholics but also the families of those alcoholics who are still not making any efforts to become sober. It helps members of the immediate family of alcoholics, but it also opens its doors to *all* family members—parents, siblings, and more distant relatives.

The members of an Al-Anon group with which the author is familiar receive from one another understanding of their problems and feelings, as well as emotional support that facilitates changes of attitude and behavior. They are given basic information about solutions to common problems, about the treatment process and about the nature of the illness of alcoholism. Shame is alleviated and hope engendered. The non-alcoholic spouses gain perspective on what has happened to their families and on the possibilities of change toward greater stability. Anxiety diminishes in an almost visible fashion. As they gain perspective on the situation, behavior tends to become more realistic and rewarding. By no means the least important effects derived from membership in Al-Anon are a structuring of what has seemed to be a completely chaotic situation and the feelings of security thus engendered.

Al-Anon has a very special part to play in the organization of those families whose alcoholic members achieve sobriety through the A.A. program. Through participation in Al-Anon's program, family members are able to have a recovering and growing experience parallel to that of the alcoholic. They, too, are surrounded by warmth, understanding, concern and support while they are recovering. In a very meaningful sense there is a sharing of the recovery that helps each individual family member to find himself and the family as a whole, to reorganize in a new and shared philosophy a way of life without alcohol.

Joan Jackson has been involved in education, research and community action in the field of alcoholism, and has written extensively about her research. A major area of interest for her has been the experiences of families of alcoholics.

AL-ANON: ALLY FOR THE HEALTH CARE PROFESSIONAL

by Kenneth H. Williams, M.D.

Physicians, nurses, social workers, counselors and other health care professionals have found the Al-Anon Fellowship to be an invaluable ally. Referral to Al-Anon can provide the distressed alcoholic family members with many unique benefits.

Education About Alcoholism

Most people in our society are poorly educated about alcoholism. Many still consider the alcoholic to be "weak-willed," and family members of alcoholics are no exception.

Family members benefit enormously from learning that alcoholism is a disease. Identifying the "family problem" helps prevent what otherwise can be an unpredictable series of worsening crises. The family learns to cope both intellectually and emotionally. Understanding the alcoholic blackout throws light on what otherwise may appear to be a totally inexplicable situation—or even outright lying. Understanding the "loss of control" phenomenon can explain the apparent "weak will."

While Al-Anon is not merely an educational tool, Al-Anon meetings and literature do provide an excellent source of information about this complex illness. Those who have lived with the problem of alcoholism have much to share about it.

Not infrequently, some individuals attending Al-Anon meetings will learn enough about alcoholism to identify themselves as alcoholic. The subsequent steps toward involvement with Alcoholics Anonymous are much easier to take with an Al-Anon background.

Destigmatization of Alcoholism

Alcoholism is still a stigmatized disease. While this makes it more difficult for the alcoholic to accept the illness, it also makes it more difficult for the family to accept the fact that alcoholism exists within it. The stigma prevents both the alcoholic and the family members from going for help, so that the associated shame and guilt will also be major roadblocks in successfully referring a prospective new Al-Anon member to this Fellowship. However, if the family learns about alcoholism, begins to accept it as an illness and sees that others can talk openly at Al-Anon meetings, the stigma slowly dissipates.

Assistance in Breaking Down Denial

Denial of the illness is a major defense for both the alcoholic and the family members. Some aspects of the denial system are based simply on lack of education. Others are bolstered by the stigma of the disease. Al-Anon can provide the family of the alcoholic not only with assistance in both of these aspects, as described above, but also with more subtle considerations of this complex psychological defense mechanism.

Newcomers hear others speak at meetings and can relate to common experiences and feelings. Denial that they have been adversely affected by alcoholism, denial of the roles they have played in the maladaptive family system, denial of the support they have given that inadvertently enabled the alcoholism to progress, can all break down. The supportive and accepting atmosphere at most Al-Anon meetings is conducive to the relaxation of defense mechanisms.

Emotional Support

Al-Anon is probably best described as a fellowship. Many family members come to their first meeting believing they are the only ones who have lived through the private type of hell that living with an alcoholic can be. The friendly faces and warm greeting may be all that nervous newcomers need to keep them coming back. As members who have been suffering in isolation find the ability to relate and share on a feeling level, close friendships grow and develop.

A Program For Living

Although to the scientifically trained health care professional. Al-Anon may at first appear superficially simplistic or, perhaps, religious in nature, it is in fact a rich and complex positive-thinking, self-help program that has no religious affiliation but is based on spiritual principles. The program has withstood the test of time and has proven to be ingeniously designed to assist family members into a more satisfying life.

Observations About Al-Anon

An Al-Anon meeting is an experience difficult to describe and is best understood through exposure. I would strongly recommend that any health care professional reading this book attend an "open" Al-Anon meeting. If the reader has a family connection with alcoholism, any Al-Anon meeting may be visited. In addition to providing a valuable professional experience, it is likely to offer valuable personal experience as well. If the reader does not qualify as being a friend or family member of an alcoholic and is thus not eligible for membership in Al-Anon, I suggest that they phone the local Al-Anon answering service (listed in the phone book), identify themselves as an interested professional and obtain information on attending an "open" Al-Anon meeting, where members welcome any interested person.

Referral to Al-Anon

Al-Anon groups are extremely diverse, comprising all socio-economic levels. Professionally speaking, my initial primary consideration in referring a family member to Al-Anon is to find a member or group with whom they might most easily identify and relate. This might mean referral to specially named Al-Anon groups which, while open to all, may be comprised primarily of men, physicians, homosexuals or adult children of alcoholics. Such specially targeted referrals may, in many instances, increase the chances that the newcomer will form a lasting attachment to Al-Anon.

However, the inexperienced health care professional should anticipate a less than enthusiastic response when recommending Al-Anon for the family members of an alcoholic. In my experience, referral to Al-Anon is just as difficult as referral to Alcoholics Anonymous. (The most difficult referral in my experience is to Alateen—especially if neither parent is in Al-Anon or Alcoholics Anonymous.)

The health care professional in whom the family members have confidence is in an excellent position to make a referral. If the professional is knowledgeable about Al-Anon, and especially if the professional has been to an Al-Anon meeting and has read some Al-Anon literature, the referral recommendation is even more likely to be acted upon.

Who to Refer

Anyone whose life is or has been adversely affected by a relationship to an alcoholic can benefit from Al-Anon membership. This certainly includes all first-degree relatives (children, spouses, siblings and parents) of alcoholics but may also include second-degree relatives (if a close or "live together" relationship exists or has existed), lovers, fiancees or close friends of alcoholics.

The professional's primary difficulty may be in identifying these individuals among their patients or clients. It is unusual for family members to present themselves for help and volunteer the information that their problem is related to the stress of an alcoholic family system. It often happens that distressed family members are not aware of the source of their discomfort. Even if the family member is aware, the professional may have to probe carefully for the information.

Family members of alcoholics present physicians and nurses with an endless variety of stress-related problems: gastrointestinal complaints, low-back pain, headaches, insomnia, anxiety, depression, etc. Social workers and counselors see the stress of the alcoholic family system in adults as deteriorating work performance, marital separation or divorce, physical and sexual abuse. Children may exhibit school or behavioral problems, hyperactivity, runaway episodes, juvenile delinquency, and a variety of psychological difficulties. Key symptoms also include being out of touch with feelings and having difficulty with trust. Indeed, the manifestations of the suffering alcoholic family member are almost endless.

In questioning any patient, it is reasonable to inquire about possible family stress. If the response is positive, the professional—remembering that alcoholism is the leading cause of family stress—may then inquire more directly about "drinking problems" or "drinking behavior that bothers you," rather than alcoholism per se. In my experience, the distressed family member does not usually know what alcoholism is.

In attempting to obtain information about possible drinking problems in the family, the professional must keep in mind that alcoholism is typically treated as "the family secret." The patient/client will probably have to develop a sense of trust in the helping professional before disclosing information never before shared with anyone outside the family. It will be especially difficult to learn about physical violence, neglect and incestuous behavior.

Summary

There has been tremendous growth in the professional recognition of problems resulting from the alcoholic family system. The health care professional astute enough to recognize individuals in distress as a result of their alcoholic family experience is in a unique position to refer them to other sources of help. Al-Anon should be the professional's primary resource.

Dr. Williams is in private practice, working with the Newmann Center for Addictive Diseases at St. Joseph Hospital in Reading and is Substance Abuse Unit Director at the Northwestern Institute in Ft. Washington, Pennsylvania. He is on the Executive Committee of the American Medical Society on Alcoholism and is a class A Trustee of Alcoholics Anonymous.

Al-ANON AND GOOD MENTAL HEALTH

by Daniel J. Anderson, Ph. D.
&
Harold A. Swift, A.C.S.W.

What is meant by good mental health? The experts use expressions like "feeling confident and comfortable about oneself," "being interested in others and considerate," and "able to meet the demands of life." In talking about family life, words like supportive, cooperative, flexible, tolerant and dependable describe the ideals to strive for. Of course, people fall short of these ideals in their personal lives and in their families, but some achieve them now and then, at least in part. For many living with the problem of alcoholism, however, these moments of personal satisfaction in a pleasant family life are infrequent and tentative. There is little consistent joy in life—sometimes none at all.

From the viewpoint of the mental health professional who works with alcoholic families, the Al-Anon Family Groups are a blessing, because they provide a model program, freely available almost everywhere, which addresses the emotional needs of these troubled people with accuracy, simplicity and thoroughness. Obviously, some need additional counsel, but the Al-Anon Family Groups must be recognized as the mainstay of help.

Al-Anon offers something a therapist cannot provide: the special support and comfort of fellowship with others who understand alcoholism in its many manifestations. Sharing experiences with others and taking hope from them offers relief from the anguish and self-doubt, from the bitterness and hurt, and from the fears that often torment alcoholic families. Ernest Kurtz is writing about Alcoholics Anonymous when he describes one central dynamic of fellowship that also describes the fellowship of Al-Anon. He says that when these people meet together, they experience the "shared honesty of mutual vulnerability openly acknowledged." The frequent repetition of this experience at AA and Al-Anon meetings, coupled with efforts to live at home according to the Twelve Step Program, is reassuring and healing to troubled spirits in a way that defies explanation. They regain the ability to reflect on their lives—not only on their problems but also on solutions.

Once the fellowship has begun to give people hope and a renewal of faith, Al-Anon members make a dramatic change in their perception of alcoholism. Instead of focusing on the person who most obviously needs help, Al-Anon urges family members to examine *themselves*: how have they unwittingly become their own worst enemies (and the alcoholic's, too) as they have struggled to help someone else? This process of self-examination is easy for some: the Al-Anon message is like a light turning on. It's a long slow process for most family members, however, to learn how their anxieties, anger, resentments and preoccupation with someone else's problem have aggravated and maintained it rather than solving it. Throughout this process they must be constantly reminded through the Al-Anon fellowship that they have always done the best they could do at the time. Families need to be reminded that almost anyone would have done many of the same things, given the situation they were in. Helping people to pull themselves out of these situations is the mission of Al-Anon, and this is done without recrimination toward the alcoholic, or toward the family or toward the past. To quit blaming is essential.

Once family members have re-learned how to reflect on what's happening in their lives, once they can be both realistic and optimistic at the same time and once they have begun to see with some accuracy how they themselves have become involved in the problem of alcoholism, Al-Anon encourages its members to follow the Twelve Step guidelines that help them to be less anxious and more thoughtful as they go about their daily lives. Who could ask more from a program for restoring good mental health?

But Al-Anon is much more than a good mental health program. The Fellowship, together with the universal principles for right living that it espouses, can lead people to a renewed appreciation of life. The title of this book is most apt: Al-Anon *does* face alcoholism, without blinking. Living life fully and joyfully is the goal of the Al-Anon program.

One key element in taking a new approach to life is the basic concept of *detachment with love*. This is ground where the professional must tread lightly and where the fellowship of Al-Anon can move more confidently. Al-Anon urges its members to understand that they are powerless to change another person. This is a very hard thing to realize fully, especially when that person is in big trouble and everyone knows it. That they can love an alcoholic—even enough to leave if that has to be—but that they can't make the alcoholic be different, is a terrible truth and a wonderful one at the same time.

Paradoxically, detachment with love helps people discover their own spiritual lives as they realize that they too are in the hands of a Higher Power. The spirit of fellowship is essential to a process of learning, and understanding can be seen in the faces of Al-Anon members.

Detachment helps people to know a higher form of love than they may have known when they were preoccupied with the alcoholic, always trying to second-guess the next move, the next disaster. Trying to keep the alcoholic out of trouble, cheering him up, encouraging him to pull himself together—all these are loving things to do. But isn't a greater love required to help only when it is truly helpful and, finally, to allow the alcoholic to know the consequences of his or her own behavior? Al-Anon thinks so. How is it possible to draw the line between the things to be done to make the situation better and the things that cannot be done? Al-Anon urges its members to ponder this question in their hearts.

Love turns into desperation when people are unable to recognize the point at which, in helping others, they have taken too much upon themselves. Al-Anon asks its members to stop obsessively devising new strategies for dealing with the alcoholic. Instead, members are reminded at every meeting in the Serenity Prayer to consider the difference between the things they can do and the things they cannot do in helping others—especially those they love most.

As this essential difference is defined, family members begin to feel more confident about themselves and, therefore, more patient with their loved ones, more tolerant of them. They become better able to make good decisions about their lives.

Daniel J. Anderson is President and Director of the Hazelden treatment center in Minnesota. He has been active in the alcoholism field for more than 30 years and is a speaker at national and international conferences.

Harold Swift is Administrator of Hazelden and a member of the faculty of St. Louis University School of Social Work. He is a member of the Professional and Technical Advisory Committee for the Joint Commission on Accreditation of Hospitals as well as a board member of ADPA and NAATP.

PROFESSIONAL AND AL-ANON COOPERATION IN THE TREATMENT OF ALCOHOLISM

by Betty Reddy, C.A.C.

Great progress has been made by professionals during the past 10 or 12 years in expanding the treatment of alcoholism to include the family. Yet the difficulty in admitting the existence of the problem—the outstanding symptom of the family ill-ness—still prevents many people from seeking treatment. Until recently, the major focus was on the alcoholic, with mini-programs added for their families. In the past few years, though, many professionals have recognized the need for treatment that addresses the family's symptoms; primary programs for families are being provided now in many places.

Al-Anon Family Groups, which include Alateen, have been helping families of alcoholics since the 1940's, providing the most direct and continuous help for families and friends of alcoholics. The word "family member" is used here to imply anyone whose personal life has been negatively affected by another person's drinking; this includes relatives, colleagues and friends. With statistics indicating that approximately 40 to 50 million Americans are affected by alcoholism, it would seem that Al-

Anon should be 4 to 5 times as large as A.A. Instead, the membership is only about two-fifths the size. It is obvious that, despite advances in professional services, many family members are not being reached at all.

Much has been accomplished in helping alcoholics toward recovery in the last 15 years. The success rate has been raised by early intervention, motivation into treatment and continuous followup. It has been proven that alcoholics don't have to "hit bottom" to get well, but rather need to be in a situation where treatment is accessible.

These same concepts are equally important to the treatment of families. For wherever families remain uninvolved in their own recovery program, the seeds of the illness continue to be passed on to the next generation. Every professional alcoholism program should have as its objective introducing the family members to Al-Anon and helping them to avail themselves of its support. Families need to learn of the illnesss in a gentle, easy to accept but forthright manner; they need to identify their own experience of the illness and accept their own need for a recovery plan. Al-Anon should be the main aftercare resource for families, as Alcoholics Anonymous is for alcoholics.

For family members, alcoholism causes a progressive inability to predict their own behavior because of the growing preoccupation with and reaction to another person's drinking. Generally speaking, if a person is wondering whether alcoholism is the problem, it probably is. Family members need to hear that the emotions they feel are a normal reaction to alcoholism. Frequently they experience a free-floating but pervasive fear. They are afraid of the alcoholic's reactions and are prepared to settle for "peace at any price." They worry about bills, accidents and job losses (the alcoholic's and, in some cases, their own). As they attempt to deal with the erratic, irrational behavior of the drinker, they become confused and increasingly guilty and preoccupied. As their lives become compulsively centered on try- ing to get the alcoholic to stop drinking through unsuccessful at- tempts to manipulate and control, most of their actions only enable the alcoholic to continue the drinking. Family members are caught in a cycle of repetitive non-helpful behavior that leaves them frustrated, angry and alone. They feel helpless and hopeless.

Manifesting these feelings, attitudes and actions, together with a lack of understanding of the disease, families foster the hope that if the alcoholic would stop drinking, everything would be all right. Families feel that it is not their lives but the alcoholic's life that is out of control. The role of the professional is to help family members break through their own denial and motivate them into a recovery process. They can ask families a few simple questions:

- Has your life been disrupted by someone else's drinking?
- Are you preoccupied with the drinking?
- Have you begun to dislike some of the things you say and do?

Any "yes" answer immediately helps them to identify how they have been affected by the disease of alcoholism.

The next requirement is for family members to learn that their recovery does not depend upon the alcoholic's. They must accept alcoholism as an illness and understand that the alcoholic cannot drink in moderation. This enables them to separate their own lives from the alcoholic's and to allow the drinker to be re- sponsible for his or her own actions. Regardless of the current circumstances, family members learn that they can become capable of making wise decisions and taking constructive action while being responsive to others. They can grow to have serenity and satisfaction with their lives and their relationships.

In the early stages of recovery, family members learn about detachment and become willing to separate their emotional lives from the alcoholic's. Often newcomers to Al-Anon feel that detachment looks like coldness or indifference. Some even think it means to separate physically from the alcoholic. Professionals can assist newcomers to understand the practical necessity of letting go, but only to move back enough so they do not interfere with the natural consequences of the drinking behavior and the need for the alcoholic to rebuild his or her own life. Family members must free themselves from the compulsion to "fix" things. The following exercise can demonstrate detachment in a small way:

> Stand in front of a full-length mirror. Get as close as you can. Notice how limited your vision and perspective are. All you can see are your own two eyes staring back at you. Notice further how this limits your ability to concentrate on other things. Now step back just a little; you can see your whole self. Your vision, perspective and ability to think have all expanded considerably.

For Al-Anon members, detachment is the culmination of applying themselves to all the steps and slogans of the Al-Anon program, especially the first step. This necessitates accepting a concept of powerlessness over another human being and over alcoholism. In order to reach the kind of detachment that Al-Anon members strive for, the individual must come to understand and accept his or her own feelings, attitudes, prejudices and actions and be committed to changing them in a healthy way.

It is obvious that issues of recovery for family members are difficult and complex. Although the outlook for recovery for families has improved considerably over the past ten or twelve years, many families are still left unmotivated and unaided. Professionals, whose help may be needed for initial treatment and during some phases of recovery, should carefully refer families to Al-Anon and support their continued active membership. Al-Anon members, on the other hand, need to be alert and receptive to the cooperation with professionals which eases the integration of family members into the Fellowship. Willing and knowledgeable cooperation on the part of each group will do much to insure that all persons affected by this serious, chronic illness have the opportunity to recover.

Betty Reddy has been a professional staff member of Lutheran Center for Substance Abuse in Park Ridge, Illinois, since 1969. She currently serves as the center's referral coordinator and is the author of articles and pamphlets on family services and on Al-Anon.

DETACHMENT AND GROWTH

by Peter Brock

One of the most wonderful aspects of the Al-Anon program is the capacity of the suggested Twelve Steps to provide guidelines for a progressively healthier and fuller life. We hear so much about the effectiveness of Al-Anon and Alateen in helping those affected by a drinking alcoholic achieve the detachment needed to deal with that painful situation that we sometimes forget the rewards the program continues to offer in long-term living. It has often been said that Alcoholics Anonymous is not only about drinking: it is also very much about living, and living a contented life. It can just as readily be said that Al-Anon is not just about not enabling or not reacting, but is also about living.

The concept of detachment provides a good example. Often professionals have difficulty understanding the true nature of detachment. It does not indicate a chasm between the Al-Anon members and the alcoholic, nor does detachment intend to convey a life of isolation from the problem drinker. Rather, detachment provides a platform for the practice of a more appropriate responsibility for oneself and others. It is in such ways that we see how the Al-Anon program is beautifully crafted to provide a proven method of approaching life.

Many of us, both Al-Anon members and professionals, are likely to feel that dealing with an alcoholic wife, husband, child, parent, lover, co-worker, or friend is dictated by that person's behavior rather than by any needs, problems, or circumstances of the Al-Anon member. If we do not recognize that both parties to a relationship have a responsibility, then we preclude the use of the Al-Anon program in its fullest applicability. Most professionals who work with families of alcoholics understand the way in which the program meets the present concerns and prepares for the future needs of each individual in dealing with various living situations, particularly with relationships.

People who have lived for any length of time in a close relationship with an alcoholic have found themselves engaged to some extent in trying to control outcomes, especially with regard to the alcoholic's drinking. It is a major adjustment to understand that one can only be responsible for one's own behavior and must therefore let go of a need to control the result — part of which involves another person's behavior. Having achieved such a major shift in perception and motivation in one area, it seems reasonable to recognize the value of practicing this principle in all one's affairs.

Many family members reach out for help, either to a professional agency or to Al-Anon, before the alcoholic in their lives has been able to accept any help for his or her problem. One of the first things any knowledgeable resource will help the concerned person understand is the need to focus on oneself rather than on the behavior of the alcoholic. Many families are in the throes of pain and confusion as they reel from one crisis to the next, feeling inextricably controlled by all the trouble and sadness that the alcoholic accumulates. They begin to feel that they have little to say about how their own life works out. Detachment is a valuable concept and tool for these people in disentangling their thinking and their reactions from the behavior of the drinker. However, the very strength of this mechanism contains some potential drawbacks. Many of us have seen, and sometimes have continued to focus on, the great value for the Al-Anon member in detachment from the alcoholic. A genuine sense of detachment can be the source of so much relief and so much change in a brief period of time that it is seen as nothing short of miraculous. What we must understand, and help the newcomer to Al-Anon to understand, is that detachment is not isolation nor should it remain focused on not enabling the sick behavior of the past. Detachment is not a wall; it is a bridge across which the Al-Anon member may begin a new approach to life and relationships in general.

As we go through life most of us engage, to some degree, in manipulation of those around us. Similarly, many of us feel a certain amount of control being exercised by others in determining the course and quality of our lives. In an alcoholic family, it is not unusual to see all the family members, including the alcoholic, veering from a highly manipulative to a highly victimized mentality. We sometimes see great amounts of energy invested in determining the truth of these charges and countercharges of exploitation/victimization within the family. In many instances it may be much less important to determine the truth of these perceptions than it is to change the dynamics that gave rise to them—in other words, the cultivation of healthy attitudes and appropriate detachment in shaping one's own thoughts and behavior.

When the active alcoholism has been dealt with—either through the sobriety of the alcoholic or through his or her removal from the immediate family environment—it becomes increasingly important to recognize the need to utilize the Al-Anon program as a guide in all one's relationships. To continue the focus on dealing with the sober and/or absent alcoholic largely or exclusively is to limit rather severely the potential for recovery of the Al-Anon member. To move our earlier parallel one step along in the recovery continuum, just as A.A. is about living more than it is about not drinking, so Al-Anon is about living more than it is about dealing with a non-drinking alcoholic. I believe that, until we can shift our focus from the interaction with the alcoholic to a broader view of our self-responsibility in approaching life, we are still in the active throes of the family illness of alcoholism.

It is much easier to characterize a relapse for an alcoholic than it is for a member of Al-Anon, but this does not mean that the phenomenon is any less real or frequent, nor is it any less recognizable to the seasoned observer than is the drinking behavior of the relapsed alcoholic. There are signals and symptoms apparent to the veteran Al-Anon member, as well as to the experienced professional, which indicate the need for a non-alcoholic to modify his or her thoughts and behavior if recovery is to continue as a progressively enhanced life. These indicators usually take the form of reverting to old habits in familiar situations and relationships. They can just as readily appear, however, in new situations and new relationships if a person is not on guard. Again, true detachment is a wonderful resource to keep one's balance between responsibility for self and responsibility to and for others. There are many occasions when we all engage in enabling destructive or inappropriate behavior in other people. This can happen in the family, in the workplace, in social settings, or anywhere else where people interact with one another. It can be done in ignorance, out of a mistaken notion of kindness or concern, or because it is easier and less threatening to the enabler. All of us, Al-Anon member and professional alike, have seen this in people around us and perhaps have discovered it in our own behavior. The danger lies not so much in what we are "causing" or "preventing" but in the resurgence of the mental attitude that we are responsible for someone's behavior and consequently for the results of that behavior. Most instances are not so obvious or dramatic as the enabling that may have gone on with the alcoholic. Nonetheless, we still need to be conscious of the potential for this unhealthy and unproductive behavior and to guard against it.

There is yet another area where I believe detachment has a central role. That is in the relationship of an Al-Anon member with a Higher Power, as each individual defines that power. Again, an appropriate level of responsibility—humility, if you will—is essential for the healthiest and most fruitful direction of spiritual growth. Probably nowhere is this dealt with more clearly and more succinctly than in the Serenity Prayer: "God grant me the serenity to accept the things I cannot change, courage to change the things I can, and the wisdom to know the difference."

With one's Higher Power, it is also essential to understand the need for responsible behavior and the acceptance of the outcomes that proceed from it. Even in this special relationship, there is often an inclination to try to manipulate the results. The Al-Anon member has come to recognize that he or she cannot control the drinking of an alcoholic. Yet many are still unable to see that prayers couched in terms of specific requests and specific results may often be just as self-defeating and just as unhealthy as is trying to control another's behavior by reactions and plans. Most people in Al-Anon come to understand the futility of attempting to control another person's behavior through their own behavior. They understand the need to focus on themselves, on the way they are thinking and acting, rather than attempting to control and dictate to the other person. How much more obvious the thought should be (and yet how seldom it is!) that one cannot control one's Higher Power. In using the slogan "Let Go and Let God," how often is added a silent tagline, "but let God do it this way." There is often a failure to recognize the resurgence of an old pattern of destructive behavior in what most of us see as a positive reliance on the spiritual relationship.

Similarly, while many Al-Anon members recognize the value of detachment in dealing with family members, friends, business associates and others, they may shy away from the application of detachment in their relationship with their own spirituality and the embodiment of that in a Higher Power. I believe that, as an Al-Anon member pursues and grows in the practice of the recommended Twelve Step program of recovery, the Serenity Prayer comes to embody the only request which needs to be made of that Higher Power. If one can determine with increasing readiness and accuracy when it is appropriate to accept and when it is appropriate to act, one is certainly committed to growth along spiritual lines. If one can concentrate on a responsible approach to the journey of life, the Higher Power will take responsibility for the destination. To have such an attitude is the ultimate gift of Al-Anon, not only to its members, but to all of us who are able to embrace this simple, powerful, universal program.

Peter Brock is the President of the Johnson Institute in Minneapolis, Minnesota. He has written articles and pamphlets on the family process of intervention, prevention and the family nature of alcoholism.

AL-ANON BENEFITS
HOSPITAL IN-PATIENTS

by John D. Vetrano, M.A.

For several years an Al-Anon Group has been meeting at a hospital family treatment facility and has been well attended. The Al-Anon Group has grown in importance to family and staff alike. With this growth, some interesting facts about the group have come to light. Not only family treatment patients, but also general hospital patients, visitors and hospital personnel all take advantage of the Al-Anon Institutions group that Al-Anon members have made available at the hospital.

For many reasons people make an emotional connection in a "safe" hospital environment. Therefore, some people who were apprehensive about or resistant to Al-Anon involvement have begun participating at the Institutions group. Some report that this involvement later helps them make a successful transition to a home group in their own community.

Al-Anon has also cooperated by respecting our family treatment goals while reenforcing Al-Anon traditions. This has resulted in a relationship of mutual trust and respect between the professional staff and Al-Anon members.

Based on our positive experiences, I believe that Al-Anon, together with the patient and family treatment program, provides comprehensive exposure to all available resources and aids in recovery.

John Vetrano is Chief Therapist for the alcohol treatment unit at St. Joseph's Hospital, Mt. Clemens, Michigan.

STRAIGHT TALK FROM A DOCTOR

by Abraham Twerski, M.D.

The telephone rang in my office. It was Mrs. W. on the phone.

"It's terrible, Doctor," she said. "Tom has started all over again. After he came out of the hospital, he was all right for two months, and then he started drinking again, slowly at first but now it's just as bad as ever. I'm at my wit's end. I just can't take it anymore!"

"Has Tom been attending his meetings?" I asked.

"He went for the first three weeks, but then he quit. He said he didn't want to hear any more drunk stories, and that the meetings didn't do anything for him. I begged him to go back, but he wouldn't. He's set in his ways and you can't budge him. I just don't know what to do."

"How have you been doing with your Al-Anon meetings?" I asked.

"Oh, I went to two of them, but they're really not for me. I have nothing in common with other men and women there."

"Tell me, dear," I said, "Do you hear what you are saying?"

"What do you mean?" Mrs. W. asked.

"You are critical of Tom's refusal to go to A.A. meetings and you consider him bullheaded and opposed to reasoning. Yet, in practically the same breath you say about *yourself* and Al-Anon exactly the same thing he says about *himself* and A.A. I think you are avoiding Al-Anon for the same reason that Tom is avoiding A.A. Neither of you want to make the necessary changes in your own lives."

Such a conversation is not infrequent. Family members who are highly critical of the drinker for not attending A.A. see nothing wrong with their own avoidance of Al-Anon. We are all familiar with the wife, or the husband for that matter, who refuses to attend a second Al-Anon meeting: "I don't see what good it can do. I asked them for pointers on how to get my husband/wife to stop drinking, and they told me they had none and that I couldn't do anything to make the alcoholic stop. All they could do is help me with myself. But there is nothing wrong with *me. My partner's* the one who needs the help."

People involved in the A.A. or Al-Anon program are fortunate in subscribing to the fundamental principles expressed in the Serenity Prayer. The Serenity Prayer really says it all. "The serenity to accept the things I cannot change" in fact refers to everything outside of myself. There is often little I can do about *anything* else and absolutely nothing that I can do about *anyone* else. "The courage to change the things I can" refers to me. The only thing I can effectively change is myself. Most people tend to see themselves as unalterable facts. No one likes to change. It is uncomfortable to change one's lifestyle and give up some of one's own pleasures.

Nonetheless, all families could benefit from constructive changes. Indeed, the ideal family probably does not exist. In a typical family there are apt to be many problems. Budgeting is often difficult: There is just not enough money to satisfy all the wants. Daughter is having social problems and is not as popular as she would like to be. Son is having trouble with his grades at school. Overcoming these difficulties would require everyone to take a good look at themselves and make some significant changes in their lives.

Now suppose Dad drinks too much. Aha! There's the problem. The finances are in bad shape because he drinks. Daughter is unpopular because she cannot invite friends to her home lest they see father under the influence, and son cannot concentrate on his studies because father's drunken clowning and cranky behavior torment him.

Then suppose that father attempts to sober up. Wonderful! This is the miracle everyone has been waiting for.

But is it really all that wonderful? With the absence of the alcoholism that served as a scapegoat, the other members of the family will now be compelled to look at themselves to discover the true reasons for their problems, many of which may persist. No longer can they all be blamed on Dad, for he's sober now. They might have to change some of their own ways. Perhaps mother needs to look realistically at her desires and lifestyle. Daughter might have to examine what she is doing that diminishes her popularity, and son might have to change his study habits and devote more time to his education.

In a way, life was much easier when Dad drank. And since there is always a tendency to gravitate to that which is easier, the family may unwittingly undermine Dad's recovery.

Sometimes I feel sorry for people who never had a drinking problem because they cannot benefit from the personal growth provided by AA. I feel even sorrier for the people who are living with an alcoholic and who could benefit from the personal growth available in Al-Anon as nowhere else, but are somehow unable to take advantage of it.

The most vital elements of life, such as air, are free. So is Al-Anon!

Dr. Twerski is Clinical Director of the Department of Psychiatry at St. Francis General Hospital and Medical Director of Gateway Rehabilitation Center, both in Pittsburgh, Pennsylvania. He has written articles and books on self-esteem and the role of the family in recovery from alcoholism.

WHAT CAN I DO? ASKS A DOCTOR

by William C. Van Ost, M.D., F.A.A.P.

See a cute little kid clutching his head or his stomach, hiding his real hurt... the pain in his heart.

Hear the tension in the voice of a young parent berating the nurse because the doctor is late, because a child is ill, because the bills are unpaid, because "nobody cares"... showing the tip of an unbearable rage.

Smell the stench of filthy clothes clinging to the body of a tiny victim of parental neglect.

Feel the belly of a young girl as she sobs through the tale of a pregnancy spawned by incest.

Taste the salty tears of a small child you hold in your arms and try to console while you examine bruises and welts... the results of child abuse.

These are the five senses put to the test. Seeing, hearing, smelling, feeling, tasting... "five faculties of receiving impressions through organs of the body." The physician must receive input from each of them. He must separate them and sort them. He must recombine and refit these pieces in order to find the cause of his patient's distress. A doctor cannot solve this puzzle alone. He needs help.

43

A physician needs to be told the truth; he needs to know all of the facts. Then perhaps the vital *sixth* sense—his instinct—will provide the key to the cause of this family destruction: the disease of alcoholism.

Try, if you will, to understand the physician who does not or cannot recognize these clues so obvious to some but so obscure to the rest. Perhaps he, like others who are reading this book, may never have been exposed to the grim facts of the effects of alcoholism on family, friends and the entire community.

It is tragic but true that most medical schools have offered very little training in the disease of alcoholism over the years. Today, with around 120 schools in existence, only 40 offer courses that would remotely prepare a doctor to deal with the disastrous physical, psychological and social results of alcohol abuse. In these schools only a few precious hours are devoted to a disease that claims more than 10 million victims "hooked" on a socially acceptable but addictive drug. With so little training, what role can we ask a family physician to assume when he encounters the active alcoholic or the damaged family?

Consider the facts. On any given day, according to estimates, more than half the hospital beds in the U.S. are occupied due to the direct or indirect effects of the nation's number one health problem: alcohol abuse and alcoholism. The United States has a minimum of 40 million spouses, children and others affected by this country's 10 million alcoholics. Consider that, of 30,000 reported cases of child abuse and 2,000 child deaths resulting from abuse reported in 1976, 34.4% involved alcohol. Consider that alcohol is a factor in 20% of all divorces, and alcohol abuse accounts for 40% of cases in family court. These facts are brutal, but true.

Most physicians are quite good at treating the effects of alcohol on the body. We are skilled at treating pancreatitis or liver disease caused by drinking. But when it comes to telling patients of their probable alcoholism, most doctors feel they are making an accusation, not a valid diagnosis. Even today, one hears the term "reformed alcoholic." Do we talk about a "reformed cardiac" or "reformed diabetic"? Alcoholism is not a moral problem. It is an illness, a disease.

If most physicians are at a loss when attempting to give guidance to concerned families and friends, what can you do? What can I do? How can we help solve the dilemma?

In spite of the doubts, suspicions and fears, this book should assure you that there *is* help. Everyone can participate. Too often the family that has been abused and ashamed closets the truth and denies the root cause of its unbearable pain. Give your doctor a chance to help: *tell* him all the facts.

More and more physicians have found that the best pathway to physical, mental and spiritual recovery for the alcohol-damaged family is through sincere participation in Al-Anon and Alateen. But should your doctor indicate that he has had no exposure to these fellowships, share your appreciation of these "pathways of hope." Write to him, send him the literature and talk with him about the wisdom, courage and serenity that can be found by participating in these programs.

Those fortunate physicians who have already been acquainted with Al-Anon and Alateen must share *their* knowledge with their untrained colleagues, using all the means at their command. We *can* resolve our dilemma. We *can* show that we really care for the alcoholic and that we care equally about their families. Together, through the fellowship of Al-Anon and Alateen, we can offer the means to bind up the wounds.

Dr. Van Ost, a private practitioner in Englewood, New Jersey, is a Spokesperson for the American Academy of Pediatrics, and President of its New Jersey Chapter. He is a co-founder of the Van Ost Institute for Family Living, a non-profit outpatient facility for alcoholics and their families.

THE CLERGY AND
THE FAMILY DISEASE

Alcoholism does not appear, progress or maintain itself in isolation. It is a family disease, and those who live in the presence of an alcoholic become quite damaged themselves. Not only are they emotionally involved with a sick person, as indeed they would be with any member of the family who becomes ill, but with alcoholism their involvement is deeper because this disease damages physically, mentally and spiritually all those who are touched by it. Confronted with these terrible effects, the clergyman can be of great help to family members if he is sensitive to the true nature of the problem and able to deal with it straightforwardly.

Counseling Spouses of Alcoholics

Often the wife or husband of an alcoholic, even though desperate for help, will refuse to acknowledge alcoholism as the problem. The sense of shame, the constant tension of not knowing what will happen next, and the resulting withdrawal and isolation contribute to making the spouse of an alcoholic difficult to approach. If counseling is to be effective, a clergyman usually has to lay the groundwork by explaining that alcoholism is a disease. In working with the spouse, he usually has a dual task: to secure an open admission of the existence of alcoholism and to help the individual realize that both partners are deeply affected by the disease.

One of the greatest services an enlightened clergyman can perform, once the presence of alcoholism has been acknowledged, is to suggest that the non-alcoholic partner take advantage of the tremendous resources of help and healing available in Al-Anon. The clergyman should himself be well enough acquainted with the program to understand its great potential for transformation and to overcome the conventional resistance of the non-alcoholic to "going public" with the problem. Once the spouse of an alcoholic has found the acceptance and understanding of the Al-Anon fellowship, emotional and spiritual growth begins, and the clergyman can observe a marvelous metamorphosis that in itself is a joy and an inspiration. The Al-Anon program teaches a change in attitude and style of living, and members of the fellowship who thus develop new priorities for their lives are able to make a significant spiritual contribution to any religious community.

In counseling the family affected by alcoholism, one of the most difficult tasks for the clergyman is to refrain from giving well-meaning but too-specific advice. Telling a spouse what he or she should do—in effect, making decisions for the family—is a serious mistake. If a family is led, or pushed, into a choice that is not fully accepted or believed in, the whole situation may be made immeasurably worse. Indeed, if the clergyman attempts to intervene or thwart the normal process of events, he may well prevent the very crises out of which a vital decision might be made that could even lead to a permanent solution.

The role of the pastoral counselor is not to make decisions but rather to interpret what is happening. However much the counselor may wish to change a given situation, the only valid way he can do this is by learning and interpreting what is taking place (at the same time providing emotional support), and then allowing the family members to make their own choices and act out their own roles in the drama of life. Naturally, this difficult principle applies even to the family's decision to accept the help of Al-Anon, which cannot be forced on anyone, however needy.

This is not, however, to minimize or belittle the actual contribution of the counselor. The family's frequent lack of understanding of the forces at work in the interactions of alcoholism demands considerable insight and interpretation on the part of the counselor—and this amounts to much more than just passive listening. Such counseling is, in effect, two persons working together to explore and resolve a problem.

Indeed, one-to-one counseling on a purely individual basis is the pastoral counselor's most productive approach in this circumstance, rather than any concerted attempt at marital counseling in its conventional form. For the purpose of counseling a non-alcoholic spouse is *not* to preserve the relationship but to assist that individual toward recovery. Maintaining this focus requires great concentration and restraint on the part of the counselor, since the prospect of separation is the eventuality that most troubles many clergymen—and often tempts them to intervene inappropriately. The fact is that alcoholism rarely runs its course without some period when the partners in any alcoholic relationship are separated: a few months, even years, or permanently. Separation is so common—and so often misunderstood—that it deserves special discussion in any remarks addressed to counselors.

If separation occurs, there should be no attempt to promote quick, easy reconciliation. Indeed, considerable harm has been done by clergymen who have intruded on this process and have forced the non-alcoholic partner to return too soon.

Separation, when properly motivated, can spur the beginning of recovery from alcoholism, which then may be followed by a genuine reconciliation and the establishment of the first real relationship a couple has ever had. The basic problem is not that a couple may be separated for the moment if the disease is not brought under control, but that the marriage may end tragically in death or divorce. The only way for this progressive disease to be arrested is for the drinking to stop. If remaining in the relationship means, in effect, enabling the drinking to continue, the non-alcoholic partner is completely justified in considering separation, not only for the obvious personal benefit but also as a means of forcing the alcoholic to face reality and, perhaps, find recovery.

It is possible for a spouse to leave an alcoholic in love, rather than waiting for that love to be destroyed. No partner should be condemned for refusing to join an alcoholic in a suicide pact, and continued drinking for an alcoholic is exactly that—a form of slow, unconscious suicide. Moreover, in some instances, continuing to live with a drinking alcoholic may be so destructive that the family may be irreparably damaged. Still loving the alcoholic, but motivated by love of self and love of children, a spouse may separate to protect the entire family.

Strangely enough, alcoholism is the only major illness in which separation does not occur, as a matter of course, through normal medical procedures. If a husband becomes mentally ill, hospital care is initiated when the illness becomes severe. When a husband is incapable of caring for a tubercular wife, hospitals are available. In both instances, separation is effected by pro-longed treatment and hospitalization. Yet when the non-alcoholic spouse is unable to cope with the physical and mental effects of alcoholism, it is often found that private hospitaliza-tion is beyond the family's financial needs or that public facilities are utterly inadequate. Most spouses are left to fend for themselves, and when they do seek help, rarely is it available in the form needed. We must either accept separation for the well-being of the family, or provide adequate care for the alcoholic.

Finally, it should be acknowledged that, in the majority of cases, separation has actually been a fact of life for some time. During the worst stages of alcoholism, the effects of the disease have caused the alcoholic partner to fail in many areas of re-sponsibility. Indeed, his or her ability to "love, honor and cherish" may long since have vanished. The separation resulting from alcoholism really occurs when the alcoholic is unable or unwilling to keep the marriage vows (or to participate responsibly and lovingly in the relationship).

Counseling Children of Alcoholics

By far the largest group afflicted by alcoholism are the children. A conservative estimate puts their number at 12 or 13 million, many of whom are in danger of becoming alcoholic themselves without counseling and appropriate help.

It is earnestly recommended that the clergyman or pastoral counselor refer any youngster between the ages of 12 and 18 to Alateen, the program for teenagers which is an outgrowth of Al-Anon.

The children of alcoholics are not like other teenagers. Usually they have spent years living under the same roof with an alcoholic parent and have suffered from the illness in their own way. The children have endured their parents' tantrums, dreaded their excesses and accepted their moods. Only those who have lived with this situation can know it.

Most teenagers who come to Alateen feel they are the only ones in the world who have had to endure the uncertainties of alcoholism. Most have a fairly well-developed martyr complex. Most have long since decided that their parents did not want them, do not want them, or couldn't care less about them. Most of those who come to Alateen learn for the first time as a complete revelation that alcoholism is a disease. In Alateen meetings they meet others who have endured similar feelings of rejection. They meet those who have learned to cope with embarrassing situations because one or both of their parents are drinking. In Alateen, the young share experiences, solve mutual problems and assist each other in being the fine young people they are meant to be—and can be.

The clergyman or pastoral counselor may have to overcome certain obstacles in referring a youngster to Alateen. One of the greatest hindrances is parents. Many do not want their children to attend Alateen even though both parents may be enjoying the benefits and blessing of AA and Al-Anon. It is a great mistake for parents to underestimate their youngsters' seriousness of purpose, their earnest desire to learn how to live successfully despite the difficulties of alcoholism. The clergyman can do much to reassure the parents of the benefits of Alateen to the whole family and can allay their fears and embarrassment that the children have also been seriously affected by the family disease of alcoholism.

Teenagers themselves may show a reluctance to attend Alateen. They too are unwilling to face the difficult feelings associated with the drinking. It is easy to cite conflicts with homework, preparation for tomorrow's classes or a sports program as the reason why attending an evening Alateen meeting is impossible. Transportation is another problem, as most Alateens do not drive, and walking the streets at night can be dangerous. A solution to such problems may be in holding an Alateen meeting at the same time as an Al-Anon or A.A. meeting. In this way, getting help can be seen as a family affair. Without it, the emotional disturbance caused by having an alcoholic parent can have long-lasting effects. A clergyman should urge teenagers with alcoholic parents to attend Alateen as a top priority.

Conclusion

Virtually all members of families affected by alcoholism suffer from serious physical, emotional and spiritual problems. Fortunately, those who seek help through Al-Anon and Alateen are able to face those problems with new strength and perspective. They learn not to speculate fearfully about the future or brood over the past, instead dealing with each day—often each minute—as the time that really counts in their lives. Living one day at a time frees them to cultivate a new relationship with the God of their understanding, which in turn reinforces their sense of wholeness and acceptance.

As this spiritual growth occurs, they develop a greater sense of community, no longer isolating themselves because they feel hopeless and afraid. They discover a sense of concern for others, and seek to find ways to express that concern: their ministry to others has begun. Clearly, such individuals are an important spiritual resource for any religious community, in an era when so many people are fearful about the future.

This article was excerpted from "Pastoral Counseling of Wife and Family" and "Why Alateen?" in Al-Anon Faces Alcoholism, *1st Ed., with additional thoughts contributed by Rev. Gene Geromel, author of several books on pastoral care and pastor of St. Bartholomew's Church, Swartz Creek, Michigan; and Rev. Joseph Martin, co-founder of Father Martin's Ashley, an alcoholism treatment center in Havre de Grace, Maryland.*

ALATEEN, WHY REFER?
A PSYCHOLOGIST'S VIEWPOINT

by Patricia O'Gorman, Ph.D.

Clinicians routinely and frequently come into contact with children of alcoholics. Given the fact that there are an estimated 28 million children—adolescent, young adult, adult and elderly offspring of alcoholics, it would be difficult not to. The 28 million figure could be an under-estimate, since a recent national survey found one-third of all households reporting that alcoholism was a major health problem affecting the whole family.*

This demonstrates that clinicians have a major responsibility in assessing whether their clients have been affected by the alcoholism of a parent or other close relative (such as a brother or sister) and must be knowledgeable about community alcoholism resources for family members. For clinicians dealing with the adolescent, the major community resource will be Alateen, the teenage component of Al-Anon.

Alateen Groups function as peer information and support groups. Adult members of Al-Anon act as adult sponsors. The

---

*Alcohol Abuse in America, November 1982, The Gallup Organization, Inc.

role of the sponsor is to facilitate the group organization or, at times, group discussion. Groups elect a member to be the chairperson, and this person decides on a topic and conducts the meeting. Group meetings often focus on one of the Twelve Steps or Twelve Traditions of Al-Anon. Discussions involve each member, in turn, relating his or her personal experience to the topic. In this manner, interactive dynamics are minimized as members focus primarily on the topic rather than the person speaking. Members are often encouraged to participate in more than one group, although experience indicates that adolescents in particular will only attend the group with which they feel the greatest bond.

Alateen can be of great assistance to the therapist who is working with a child of the alcoholic. Not only will Alateen educate the adolescent about the disease of alcoholism, but it can serve as a major therapeutic resource in uncovering issues that need to be dealt with in psychotherapy. Further, it has the benefit of introducing the adolescent to an empathic and supportive peer group.

Primary Advantages of Alateen to the Adolescent

1. Dealing With an Alcoholic Relative:
   The principal reason for referral to Alateen is the fact that the adolescent is confronting issues arising from close contact with an alcoholic parent or close relative. This is usually manifested by being either protective of the alcoholic or non-alcoholic parent, being resistant to seeing the alcoholic or non-alcoholic parent as having a problem, or being enraged at one or more parents. Often adolescents have begun to define themselves as being the major

problem within the family setting. Alateen assists them in confronting and dispelling this fallacy.

2. Learning About Alcoholism:

   In Alateen adolescents exchange feelings about living with an alcoholic parent or close family member. They are free to explore the complex disease of alcoholism, as it affects them, as they share with peers the experience and effects of growing up in an alcoholic family situation. The sponsor acts as a non-threatening but knowledgeable adult to whom they can turn for help in understanding, for example, how it feels to be the non-alcoholic partner, how the loyalties to spouse and children may conflict, or what it is like to grow up and leave an alcoholic home.

3. Overcoming Isolation and Learning Social Skills:

   Another reason for referring an adolescent to Alateen is that in the process of being with a group of youngsters the adolescent's isolation, fear and embarrassment will begin to diminish. Further, Alateen enables adolescents to learn communication and social skills by encouraging openness with peers about this crucial and painful subject. One of the problems for adolescents from alcoholic homes is that, on their own, they are often unable to find peers to whom they can freely speak about their alcoholic parents. The more obsessed they become with the alcoholic, the more they are likely to withdraw from peer involvement.

Secondary Advantages of Alateen to the Adolescent

1. Learning From Peers:

   Information on alcoholism is covered from a viewpoint impossible to replicate in an individual psychotherapeutic session. Information on alcoholism is learned from peers. Adults are there to offer structure and guidance, but not necessarily to be the main source of information. Adolescence is a time when youngsters learn most readily from their peers. Adolescents view information received from peers as more often being of value than information received from adults.

2. Having Information Repeated:

The structure of the Alateen group allows the same piece of information to be covered from many different viewpoints. This allows more time for the adolescent to be able to come to terms with the information, emotionally. There is a give and take of information that allows the adolescent who is having more difficulty with one particular aspect to keep coming back to it, either within the formal meeting structure or afterwards with a peer or with one of the adult sponsors.

3. Learning In a Safe Atmosphere:

Groups are run in a non-threatening and supportive manner. This allows adolescents to discuss issues freely with each other. There is no ridicule. It is also permissible not to understand and to ask for more help.

4. Learning More About Feelings:

Groups foster a decrease in intellectualization, and an increase in the focus on feelings. The structure of the groups allows its members to move from acquiring an information base to focusing on how they feel about the information that is given. This is important because this type of process goes far beyond what could normally be covered within a school program. School programs are, in most communities, the only other source of information on alcoholism open to the adolescent.

5. Speeding the Psychotherapeutic Process:

Change and the acceptance of personal responsibility are major themes of Alateen. Alateen, through the very structure of meetings, allows adolescents to begin to break down their resistance to viewing themselves in a more objective manner. A personal inventory is taken as a regular part of the program. The program helps young people begin to accept personal responsibility. As a result they experience an increase in control over their own lives, as they give up the control they never really had over the alcoholic and non-alcoholic parent or any other alcoholic relative. The themes of change and responsibility are reinforced throughout the meeting, encouraging the individual to become more self-reflective.

6 Having Peer Support To Look At Personal Alcohol and Drug Usage:

Within the group another concern may be the adolescent's own alcohol or drug usage. While this is not the primary focus of Alateen, the fact that members are trying to understand parental alcohol use tends to promote their examination of their own alcohol and drug usage. In this manner an adolescent may obtain peer support for curtailing the beginning of unhealthy alcohol or drug use patterns.

7. Learning Leadership Skills:

Through this peer-oriented experience, the young person may begin to learn leadership skills. The structured peer learning, the need to have a chair for the group who decides on topics and leads discussion, and the fact that as a secondary gain the person masters key facts and then goes on to share them with others, all combine to strengthen leadership skills. In this manner, self-concept is enhanced, as feelings are re-defined.

8. Secondary Advantage of Alateen to the Therapist:
As Alateen focuses the adolescent on dealing with alcoholism, this can allow the therapist to comfortably move on to other related issues when the need arises. Such issues can range from poor school performance to compulsive achieving, psychosomatic illness and depression, high risk-taking behavior, difficulties with the law, and social isolation.

Role of the Therapist

1. To Be Knowledgeable About Group Location:
The therapist needs to know where Alateen groups are located, for it would clearly be disruptive to the therapeutic process to refer an adolescent to a group no longer active. If information is needed, the therapist can call Al-Anon Inter-group for a listing of active groups.

2. To Overcome Initial Resistance to Attending Meetings:
Initially many adolescents are reluctant to join a group of peers in talking about a subject that arouses fear of potential embarrassment. The role of the therapist here can be that of a knowledgeable encourager. In this process, issues dealing with fear, embarrassment, and peer problems will arise and will need to be worked through as part of the therapeutic process.

3. To Encourage Attendance At More Than One Group:
Groups can vary in their degree of meaningfulness to the

adolescent. It is important for the therapist to encourage
the adolescent to attend more than one group as a way of
ascertaining the one in which they will feel most comfortable.

4. For Therapists Who Are Adult Children of Alcoholics:
If the therapist is an adult child of an alcoholic, it is crucial
for the therapist to have come to terms with the impact of a
parent's alcoholism on his or her own life. This is a matter
of extreme importance for, in treating an adolescent who
has an alcoholic parent, the therapist will need to grapple
with many of the issues which, if unresolved from his or
her own childhood or adolescence, may well hinder the
progress of the adolescent in treatment.

Special Uses of Alateen In a Residential Treatment Facility

Alateen is now being seen as a major resource in residential
programs for adolescents. It is estimated that approximately
70% of the youngsters who come through the family court system
and are placed away from their families come from alcoholic
homes. In such cases there is often a long history of involvement
with social service and even child protective agencies. Yet it is
rare to find a family in which there has been an assessment, let
alone a referral, due to the alcoholism of a parent. Most often the
problems of the child are the only focus of the system's attention.
With the alcoholic parent still residing within the home, many
difficulties are created for both the child and the agency. Alateen
therefore can be a very effective resource in a residential treatment program. In such a setting the adolescent comes to realize
that there are many young people with similar problems. Not on-

ly are the already stated advantages of Alateen important in such a population, but participation in Alateen actually helps to make the alcoholism problem a more visible issue within the family setting.

Patricia O'Gorman is the Chief Psychologist of the Berkshire Farm Center and Services for Youth in Canaan, New York. A noted lecturer and author of educational materials concerning youth and alcohol, she maintains a private practice in East Greenbush, New York.

PROCESS OF RECOVERY:
AL-ANON AND THE ADULT CHILD

by Claudia Black, M.S.W., Ph.D.

The concept of the "adult child" is spreading rapidly and is used to refer to the great number of adults who were parented in a home affected by alcoholism. Unlike people not raised in alcoholic homes, these are adults who characteristically experience greater difficulty in their ability to trust, to identify and express feelings and to ask for what they need. They experience greater difficulty in intimate relationships and are more prone to experience depression. The term "adult child" legitimizes the experiences of such a person during childhood and encapsulates a description of his or her problem as an adult. As is true for the alcoholic and the spouse, the adult child is in need of direct therapeutic intervention and the opportunity to enter a recovery process.

The self-help groups of AA and Al-Anon are often found to be the greatest resources to the recovery of the alcoholic and spouse. They not only stop the active addiction process, they offer an ongoing recovery process that becomes a very satisfying lifestyle to those who follow their Twelve Steps and Traditions. With this endorsement, it has been most natural to assist adult child clients to see Al-Anon as a viable resource for them. What is particularly beneficial about Al-Anon as a resource is that it addresses and ultimately affects the basic issues of 1) not talking; 2) not feeling; 3) not trusting; 4) guilt; 5) control; and 6) isolation.

Most young children in alcoholic families learn that it is not safe (psychologically and often physically) to talk honestly about what is occurring in their lives. This stems from a variety of reasons: shame; loyalty; uncertainty about what to say; lack of models or permission from others to talk; and fear of reprimand and negative consequences when they do speak. The support group of Al-Anon provides adult children with an arena where they are not ashamed to speak. Al-Anon is an environment in which adult children do not feel they are betraying themselves. They are given the opportunity and support to share as they choose, discovering that there are no reprimands for being honest.

Adult children usually demonstrate a great fear of feelings. They find that, through the group experience, their fears are usually put into proper perspective. In Al-Anon, people share sadness, embarrassment, anger, and fear, in the process coming to realize that they don't "fall apart." Al-Anon provides models for sharing honestly, as well as validation for the feelings when expressed. Group participants are not criticized for sharing their pain—instead, they receive understanding and empathy.

Further, Al-Anon offers adult children many dynamics that assist them in becoming more trusting. Al-Anon is a psychologically safe place; there is acceptance and unconditional love from the start, a bonding based on the common identities (trust takes time, but does occur). Al-Anon is a setting in which adult children learn that they are not responsible for things they have no control over, which lessens their guilt. They are repeatedly told, "You are not responsible." In addition, Al-Anon provides feedback allowing adult children to set appropriate limits in order to help themselves and not enable others. In the process, the adult child begins to find self-esteem.

Control is a major issue for adult children in that they have a strong need either to be in total control or to feel no control over *any* aspect of their lives. The First Step of Al-Anon immediately says, "I am powerless." For some adult children, acceptance of powerlessness means they don't have all the answers. Many adult children readily accept this and are relieved to be confirmed in their perceived helplessness. At the same time, they are also able to get appropriate feedback as to the power they do have in their lives. For other adult children, such acceptance marks the beginning of an awareness that they can no longer do it all by themselves.

The concept of acknowledging powerlessness, accompanied by the concept of "surrender," means to let go of control, which for the adult child is very frightening. Control has meant survival for the adult child. Adult children fight this because they have taken such pride in their ability to manage, achieve and perform. Although in this sense frightening, Al-Anon offers adult children a realistic perspective of their own power and helps to lessen rigidity in their need to be in control.

In treating the adult child, Al-Anon is typically indicated as a viable source for help. Nonetheless, many have gone to Al-Anon and, for various reasons, have chosen not to return. This reluctance needs to be addressed. Others are simply unaware that Al-Anon exists; many have misconceptions. Recognizing that not all adult children will choose to use Al-Anon, it is wise to insist they see it as an option before they reject it.

It is important to ask about a client's knowledge and experience with Al-Anon, but sometimes attendance at meetings is not suggested until a more trusting relationship is developed. Al-Anon may be presented as a resource the client will find helpful. If clients demonstrate any interest in Al-Anon, they can be offered a Directory and particular meetings might be suggested. If a client expresses misconceptions and negative biases toward Al-Anon, Al-Anon might be proposed at another time when the client may be better able to see this as a possible option.

New clients are typically scared, non-trusting and confused people. It has often taken all their strength to come to a counselor's office. If clients are referred to another resource of any kind too quickly, this is often perceived as betrayal. Initially, it is important to work with them so that they are less frightened, have more clarity about what it is they are experiencing, and are able to develop a greater sense of trust. Once they know they can rely upon a counselor, they know that they will not be "abandoned" or "rejected" and that they will not be hurt.

Usually, the counselor is able to establish such a rapport that clients can be directed to Al-Anon within eight to twelve weeks. It is found that adult children more easily identify with the Al-Anon meetings specifically oriented toward adult children. It is suggested they begin there for immediate identification and bonding, and that they go to several meetings before they make any decision or judgment about how they like it.

Because, at the time of this writing, adult child Al-Anon meetings are so new, most members are in the initial stages of their recovery, so it is beneficial for clients to attend a traditional Al-Anon meeting as well; usually, more long-term recovery is found there. These traditional meetings often are where adult children find their sponsors.

When a client is actively dealing with practicing alcoholics (spouse, parent, sibling, child), traditional Al-Anon meetings are strongly recommended, for it is there that clients will get the help they need to deal with immediate problems in their daily lives.

Otherwise, adult children are directed to adult child-oriented meetings, where the focus is primarily on adult child issues. Here adult children can begin to understand how their present life has been dominated by the past, can learn how to grieve the past appropriately, and can discover for the first time many valuable things they never had the opportunity to learn as children.

While many clients feel at home in their first meetings, they are cautioned that they may feel awkward. It is easily recognized that they are frightened because these meetings ask them to do what has been contrary to their sense of survival and safety—that is, talk, be honest, share feelings, and rely on others. Clients need to look for what they can identify with, and try not to focus on what it is they don't like (such as sharing problems with a group of people). It is important to try to ignore negative feelings about the group—at least in the beginning.

The most common reasons expressed by clients for avoiding Al-Anon meetings are:

1) "I want to handle my problems privately." It is understandable that the client feels vulnerable in a group of people. This is an opportunity to have them explore the disadvantages of having to cope and carry the burden all by themselves. This process usually helps to ease the pain.

2) "Home life wasn't as bad for me as it was for the other people in the meeting." When clients complain that they don't have horror stories comparable to the ones they hear, they may be reminded that the style of drinking and response to drinking may have been less blatant in their home, but that does nothing to

lessen their loss or pain. Working with clients to help them identify the loss in their life and to describe the pain they felt from
what *didn't* occur versus what did, from what *wasn't* said versus
what was, enables them more easily to identify with adult
children from more obviously disrupted homes.

3) "I don't like all that religious stuff." Many adult children
who are brought up with a specific religious preference aren't
sure they want to have a Higher Power, because if they do, it will
force them to acknowledge their anger regarding God as they
previously understood God. They perceive God as having
abandoned them, and then feel guilty for their anger. For many
adult children, it is easier to say "I don't like those meetings"
than to acknowledge their anger. Often these people have no
faith in anything other than themselves. They have been their
own best resource, and they become threatened when the concept of "turning their lives over" to a Higher Power is presented.
They often need help in exploring and discovering experiences
where they have faith in someone or something outside of themselves. This may entail helping them not to regard the world as
"all black" or "all white," instead being more flexible in how they
perceive and respond to situations.

4) "I don't like the ritual part when everyone says "hello,"
when I say my name, and when they clap after I am done speaking." When a client complains of the ritualistic clapping or
"hello," it gives us the opportunity to explore issues of acknowledgment. "I wanted to spend my whole life making sure nobody
noticed. So if I do try and change, I get scared—just let me talk,
but don't clap. I don't know how ready I am for such an
acknowledgment."

By this discussion, the client has gone one step further and is
now recognizing that he or she doesn't really want to be rejected,

but needs to ease into acceptance.

Many times, just the awareness of these feelings allows the client to feel less antagonistic. These are all very important issues to be discussed in the therapy relationship because they are not only related to the client's like or dislike for Al-Anon but are typically lifelong issues that perpetuate the problematic areas of the adult child's life.

This counselor views the resource of Al-Anon—and even more specifically, adult child Al-Anon—as an extremely valuable adjunct to the therapy process offered to clients. Clients who actively participate in Al-Anon move more quickly in their therapy process—they feel greater support and validation, are less alone. The experience of Al-Anon meetings induces adult child issues to surface that are important to focus on in therapy. Members of adult child Al-Anon take risks that assist them to be more trusting, and they are better able to identify and express feelings. It is in these abilities so essential to a client's emotional development (i.e., to trust and to feel) that the adult child begins to undertake the therapy process and ultimately establishes a basis for recovery from the past.

Claudia Black has extensive experience working with families affected by alcoholism and is the author of several books on the subject for adults and children.

ALATEEN—A WAY TO SURVIVE

by Janet Geringer Woititz, Ed.D.

"Why Alateen?" I asked the question of some young people I know who are active in the Alateen program. They answered me: "Why survive?" "Why have friends?" "Why grow?" And one of them added, less dramatically: "It's a way to get out of the house."

"Why survive?" is a profound question that reflects the intense pain and despair many of these teenagers feel when living with alcoholism. Where does a child go to get away from fighting in the middle of the night? Hiding under the covers can help block out the noise but none of the fear. How does a child please an active alcoholic when nothing is good enough, or when what was good enough yesterday is not good enough today? What does a child do when the non-alcoholic parent is bouncing off the walls or is irritable for reasons he or she doesn't understand? Day after day after day, nothing changes; there is no way out. Let's face it. Children are prisoners. They have no place to run to on their own. It is not surprising that young people often feel they cannot survive another day.

"Why Alateen?" The Alateen program helps its members to understand what is going on in their home. They learn about the disease of alcoholism, and to detach from the illness but not the alcoholic. They learn to keep things in their proper perspective. Alateens learn that they can change only themselves, that they cannot take responsibility for their parents' behavior. They learn they can survive; they use the telephone, they have sponsors and they have each other. They can even be happy. They may not be able to remove themselves physically, but they can remove themselves emotionally.

"Why have friends?" For many young people living with alcoholism, making friends is very difficult. They simply do not know how. They don't want the other kids to know what is going on in their homes. They assume that nobody else has problems and everybody is better off than they. Even if they begin to establish friendships, it's only a matter of time until they feel an obligation to invite friends home. They can't always just go to their friends' homes. What do they do then? Since they have been told by the alcoholic parent that they are not worth much anyway and since they have come to believe it, they feel they are better off not even trying to make the effort. At least they won't be rejected.

In Alateen they meet kids just like themselves who understand, who care and who have been there. They are accepted and not judged. They don't have to hide from the truth about their home lives. There is nothing more important to a teenager than his or her peer group. Outsiders are so very miserable. Children from alcoholic homes need peer group identification just as much as everybody else. Alateen gives them this. They now belong. They need never feel alone. There is no substitute for this feeling of fellowship at any time of life. but especially during adolescence.

"Why grow?" Alateen offers its members a way to work on their own personal development. It gives them an opportunity to develop self-awareness and to strive to become the sort of person they would like to be. In an atmosphere of honesty and caring, they can learn to modify those behaviors that cause them trouble and to develop their good points. How fortunate they are to have this type of opportunity. In this sense they may even become grateful for the unfortunate circumstances of their lives. For without those circumstances they might not have had the chance to be all they can be. People grow through coming to grips with adversity. Facing problems head on and dealing with them instead of avoiding them is essential to meaningful personal growth. Alateen encourages this.

"It's a way to get out of the house." Teenagers, even under the best of circumstances don't like to hang around the house. They want to be out with people their own age. That's just the way it is. Alateen offers that opportunity. It is a way out of the stressful home situation, a way to spend time in a wholesome environment.

Essentially, Alateen offers young people what Al-Anon offers adults. It is geared to their needs. In return for understanding and help, teenagers get out of it what they put in, plus the chance to grow into happy, healthy adults.

Janet Geringer Woititz, author of Marriage on the Rocks *and* Adult Children of Alcoholics, *is a therapist in private practice in Montclair, New Jersey, and conducts workshops for alcoholism counselors, mental health personnel, and educators throughout the United States and Canada.*

WHAT EVERY COUNSELOR
SHOULD KNOW

Alcoholism affects the whole family, but the non-alcoholic often presents a spectrum of problems that do not seem to involve the drinking behavior of someone else. At first glance, the primary problem may appear to be marital conflict, blocked communication, acting-out behavior of teenage children, or stressors such as unemployment, financial pressures, or psychosomatic illness. Almost without exception, family members who have lived with the complex effects of alcoholism have a well-entrenched denial system. This is the only way the non-alcoholic has been able to cope, and it is seldom understood in all its complexity by those who have not "been there."

Rather than address the peripheral effects already outlined, the counselor should refer the client to Al-Anon, for help is needed with the central dilemma of living, day in and day out, close to someone whose drinking causes or has caused distress to others. Such a family member is most effectively supported by those who have learned understanding and found ways to live with the disease effectively—in short, the men and women who make up the local Al-Anon group. The counselor should become acquainted with where and at what time this group meets. Even better, an Al-Anon member can be called upon to introduce the client to the first Al-Anon meeting. The counselor is then able to treat the client for other problems, knowing that he or she is receiving information and support regarding alcoholism.

73

What Al-Anon Is, And What It Is Not

Al-Anon is not a therapy, nor does it duplicate a counselor/client relationship. It is a worldwide, self-help organization in which each autonomous group adheres to a set of guidelines for the purpose of promoting recovery for each of its members. Membership is entirely voluntary. Each group endorses basic precepts to ensure effective operation. A simple explanation of group functioning based on Al-Anon's Twelve Traditions follows:

1. In unity lies strength. Individual recovery depends on group unity. While each member is free to express his or her own opinion, group conscience is formed by the majority view determining the direction of the group.
2. Common suffering promotes spiritual growth. No one member is different from, or more important than another. Guidance is sought through belief in a Higher Power—an outside source of strength, which is expressed through the effective development of group conscience.
3. Al-Anon's role is to provide a program of spiritual recovery. While there are pressures to conform to other recovery theories or religious views, Al-Anon resists by neither endorsing nor opposing these views.
4. Individual Al-Anon groups have complete freedom to chose their own meeting programs. This freedom carries with it the responsibility for preserving the unity of the Al-Anon program.
5. The ultimate success of Al-Anon and the recovery of its members depends on limiting the program to one purpose: helping families and friends of alcoholics. Member-

ship is open only to those who have been affected by another's drinking. (Other programs exist for those affected by drug addiction, gambling, etc.).

6. Al-Anon focuses on personal growth for the family member. Although interested professionals frequently use Al-Anon as a resource, Al-Anon's tradition of non-endorsement of other recovery programs means that Al-Anon cannot recommend professionals in return. Instead, Al-Anon maintains a separate but cooperative relationship with professionals.

7. Al-Anon declines outside financial contributions. Support for Al-Anon's worldwide services comes from the membership itself.

8. No one person is an expert on alcoholism at an Al-Anon meeting. Professionals who are also Al-Anon members should share only their own recovery.

9. Al-Anon groups require only a minimal structure. The equality of members requires only spiritual principles and logical procedures agreed upon by the majority. Special "service boards or committees" are organized to serve Al-Anon as a whole.

10. Al-Anon as a fellowship has no opinion on outside issues. Taking such a stand could divide the group or weaken the spiritual framework. Each group must function free from concerns not related to the Al-Anon program.

11. The Al-Anon program is based on attraction rather than promotion. Personal anonymity is maintained at the level of press, radio, TV and films. Al-Anon's primary purpose is to attract members by offering hope and comfort to any unhappy and confused person affected by another's drinking. Al-Anon wants others to know that support and

friendship are offered to any who feel they need help and
come to Al-Anon to find it.

12. Anonymity is the spiritual foundation of these Traditions.
It is a common problem that brings Al-Anon members
together, and subordinating the individual will to a source
of spiritual strength adds to the healing process. Other af-
filiations are left outside the Al-Anon program to encourage a greater sense of belonging among the membership.

What You Can Do As A Counselor

The fact that family members need help cannot be too strongly
stressed—they are deeply affected by alcoholism. At Al-Anon
meetings family members often see that after many years of
suffering alone, they have finally found themselves among others
who understand and welcome them. They learn where their responsibilities lie. They discover self-worth. They can grow
spiritually.

Al-Anon Family Groups have for many years played a vital role
in raising public awareness of alcoholism as a family disease. Al-
Anon provides the professional community with a well established resource for referrals, locally, nationally, and internationally.
Together, Al-Anon and the professional community can help
families of alcoholics find stability and a new way of life. Al-Anon
has some suggestions for working with family members.

1. It is beneficial to the counselor to know all he or she can
about Al-Anon. Al-Anon can be utilized fully only by those who
have gained a thorough understanding.

2. Experience shows that family members are more likely to
approach a person with an understanding of alcoholism than a

person without it. Many professionals have found workshops on alcoholism beneficial. Inclusion of Al-Anon/Alateen speakers and the availability of Al-Anon literature helps to make a workshop successful.

3. Counselors may establish a list of Al-Anon members who will introduce a newcomer to Al-Anon. There is no cost to the counselor or the client.

4. It is suggested that the counselor follow up on the client who is introduced to Al-Anon. Some people are not ready for Al-Anon. They may be turned off by a certain meeting, member or point of view they cannot accept. They need encouragement and a place to express their fears.

5. When making referrals it is necessary to keep in mind Al-Anon's Traditions. The program is only for those who have been deeply affected by someone else's drinking. There are other programs available for other needs.

Wearing Two Hats—For Counselors Who Are Also Al-Anon Members

So that the Traditions are not unknowingly violated, Al-Anon suggests the following guidelines for those of its members wearing two hats:

1. Attend Al-Anon meetings outside of the counselor's professional setting.
2. Keep therapy and sponsorship separate. A client or a patient should not be sponsored; they should be referred to Al-Anon.
3. Keep on a personal basis any recommendations of outside agencies, especially any for which the counselor may work.

4. Don't assume the role of alcoholism "expert" in the Al-Anon group. A home group should be for personal recovery only.

For Counselors Who Have, Or Have Had, The Family Disease of Alcoholism

It is urged that those in the professional community who have, or have had, alcoholism as a family problem identify and come to terms with this disease within themselves. Those who do not may be greatly disadvantaged in helping their clients.

Further Resources For Counselors

Counselors requiring further information on how they may work with Al-Anon should contact their local Al-Anon Information Office by consulting the telephone directory. Al-Anon literature is available, as are Al-Anon speakers for outside groups and contacts to whom the counselor can refer a client. Al-Anon welcomes the opportunity to work with the professional community in helping any family member who may need it.

Glossary of Al-Anon Meetings

Alateen: An Al-Anon program for the teenage children of the family—a place to share their common experience, under the guidance of an adult Al-Anon sponsor.

Closed Meetings: Meetings for members or potential members only. It is wise to assume all meetings are closed unless otherwise stated.

Open Meetings: Meetings open to anyone interested in the Al-Anon program.

Institution Groups: Meetings for those confined to an institution, they are limited to members and potential members only. They differ in that most are of an orientation nature, and the membership is transient.

Limited Access: Groups that meet in places where access is limited, such as a corporation or a military base.

Often these terms overlap, such as an Alateen Institutions Group. The most common group is a closed Al-Anon meeting in an unrestricted setting.

COUNSELORS AT A CORRECTIONAL FACILITY VIEW AL-ANON

by Frank A. Loftus
  Leo A. Boyle III
  Jon H. Zimmerman

At the Delaware Correctional Center, Al-Anon has been one of five parts of a Pre-Release Program. During the classes, two important processes took place:

1. The residents were afforded the opportunity to hear how another person had dealt with alcoholism.

2. Both residents and staff were permitted to view another person who was open and honest about feelings, failings and frailties, who did not suffer as a result of such exposure and who was able to obtain "a measure of happiness."

Counselors trained in group therapy techniques rarely reach the level of effectiveness demonstrated by the Al-Anon members who led our meetings with free and open interchange. Their humility was remarkable, especially since emphasis was placed on their non-professional status.

Not only did the Al-Anon discussion leader convey a startling honesty which revealed that he was comfortable with personal parts of his life, but he came across as a real person. This was complemented by a remarkable attitude toward events in his life. In effect, he said: "Something happened to me that hurt and changed me. What happened was not my fault, but I can do something about the changes in me, and I can stop hurting."

The warm feelings the Al-Anon members conveyed were heady stuff. They were what Carl Rogers, that great teacher of counselors, calls *unconditional positive regard.* Counselors trying to develop this feeling toward those whom they counsel should find a source in Al-Anon. Al-Alon has much to offer those who are incarcerated and those who counsel them.

Frank Loftus is Director of Pre-Release Services; Leo Boyle is a Counselor for Maximum Security; Jon Zimmerman is Counselor Supervisor for the Delaware Correctional Center in Smyrna.

A TEACHER FINDS GUIDANCE IN
AL-ANON

Let me begin with the story of one little girl who came under my care, for it is so typical of these situations.

Jenny was a cute little eight-year-old in my third grade class. She was new to the school the year I had her. Her work was satisfactory and she was very sweet, but I noticed with some wonder that even the slightest confusion, such as missing her ride home from school, made her "go to pieces." She would cry hysterically and appear completely at a loss. On many occasions she would perspire freely, and with an offensive odor, as a highly nervous adult might.

She was musical, well co-ordinated, and generally creative, as the daughter of an actor and an actress, but her artwork resembled that of a five-year-old. Her paintings were invariably of many-windowed apartment buildings, sun in the sky, lollipop trees such as you might see in an exhibit of kindergarten work.

As I observed her closely, there were definite indications of some problem in her listlessness, daydreaming, withdrawal, constant need for praise and reassurance, and panic at minor changes in routine. She seemed to have difficulty with verbal communication. Other children talked freely of their life at home; she avoided any mention of her parents as though it were something that could not safely be talked about.

One morning after assembly, her mother came up to the classroom "just to say Hello." This visit gave me an inkling of what the problem might be. My impression that she had been drinking was confirmed by a strong smell of liquor. About a month later, at a parent-teacher tea in mid-afternoon, I again noticed an alcoholic flush and liquor on her breath. Soon after, one of the other parents told me that Jenny's mother was an alcoholic.

This is a difficult situation for a teacher. To the family, she is an outsider, not permitted to take any step toward correcting a problem that is clearly damaging a little child. I did the only thing I could—tried to help Jenny by creating a school situation that would offset, to some degree, the home problem.

Through the regular channels of school discipline I attempted to bring a pattern of order and regularity into her life. Where parental guidance was obviously haphazard, lacking direction and consistency, I tried to have school offer her every possible opportunity to meet and work out problems in ways that were within her capabilities.

The school can and should play a dual role in the life of the child from an alcoholic home. It must not only provide discipline, education and adjustment to group living, but the individual teacher should, if she can, add the love and security that build self-confidence.

Because of the abnormal situation, I felt it my job to help Jenny meet her problems as they occurred, to teach her to evaluate them in relation to the world outside the home, and to solve them in a satisfying and realistic manner. I tried to keep Jenny functioning in a normal way, to prevent her from feeling so overwhelmed that she would want to escape into fantasy or apathy. Giving her extra responsibility helped to build her confidence and independence.

Although Jenny's mother continued to drink, the child showed marked improvement. Encouragement and praise made her aware of her own value. Giving her one of the leading parts in our class play did her a great deal of good. I put her in charge of small work groups within the class to give her a sense of importance. During moments of stress, I reminded her that the "crisis" was only a minor matter, to help her achieve a sense of proportion. I'd explain that it was not "the end of the world" and that she need not worry about tomorrow.

Although she did not fulfill her potential in her classwork, her grades did improve, and her creative endeavors, so often a measure of a child's state of mind, showed much greater freedom of expression by the close of the school year.

I had had the usual training for my work as a teacher, but this training does not stress such unusual problems as I encountered in working with Jenny. The modest gains I made with her were due to my knowing something about alcoholism through Al-Anon. And this was due to mere chance. A friend who teaches in the same school had a brother whose alcoholism was bringing disaster to the family. She often confided in me and I became sufficiently intrigued that I asked to go to an open Al-Anon meeting with her. I remember sitting next to a troubled woman who asked me who in my family was the alcoholic. She was astonished when I told her no one, and explained why I was interested. "I realize," I said to her, "that Al-Anon is a Family Group, but I'm sure many people are confronted in some way with this problem, without having alcoholism in the immediate family."

"That's true," she agreed. "I never thought of it that way before, and isn't it wonderful to be able to think that the title Family Groups can be applied to the whole human family! How much help you'll be able to give those children just from being able to recognize the problem and help strengthen them to meet it."

Needless to say, I am by now no stranger to Al-Anon, and much that I have learned has helped me start at the outer edge, so to speak, to offset alcoholic damage that is being done a long way from my classroom.

Perhaps it will be helpful to others in my situation to have me summarize what I have learned of Al-Anon principles to them.

The children of alcoholic parents present special problems in behavior and attitude. Not only are they emotionally affected by the alcoholic, most often the father, but they are affected by the anxieties of the nonalcoholic parent who is trying to cope with the situation. In fact, the nonalcoholic parent can often be the major disturbing factor.

Sometimes the child is hardly aware of the alcoholic parent's drinking, especially if it is the father who is away during the day and who may do his heavy drinking late at night. The child is made aware of the problem by the mother while the father is away from home. By being thus exposed to it at second hand, the child may respond out of all proportion to the threat to the family's well-being. Many alcoholic fathers actually radiate warmth and a sense of devotion which the child contrasts with the disapproval of the mother who may share her disturbed feelings with the child, conveying to him that it is only because of her that the family is able to survive. The child may see the mother's angry recriminations turn the father's amiable mood into anger and violence. Unable to evaluate the situation, unwilling to blame either parent, the child withdraws into a noncommittal attitude that makes it difficult to communicate. It is this attitude, carried over into the classroom, that should warn the teacher that there is a problem at home.

It is usually easier to detect the child from a home where the mother is the alcoholic. The general appearance of the child, a lack of attention to dress and even a general debility because of poorly supervised eating and sleeping regimen, can alert the teacher that a problem exists.

The symptoms of a child from an alcoholic home may differ

very little from those of a child from any other disturbed home environment. The main difference appears to be a breakdown in verbal communication. Exposed to a fluctuating conversational level at home, ranging from morose silence to wild ravings, the child becomes more and more withdrawn.

In normal early childhood, much of a child's talk concerns his home life—parents, pets, friends and activities. The child from an alcoholic home soon learns that most of what he sees and hears at home cannot be safely discussed outside. He or she learns early to censor conversation to avoid mention of the alcoholic scenes at home, a censorship that spreads to other areas of conversation. The child is abnormally wary about thinking before speaking. This, in the uninhibited world of children, soon leaves him or her behind in the carefree verbal give-and-take.

When the problem of alcoholism is suspected, what should be the role of the teacher, the school social worker, or whoever is in contact with the child?

It may be cautiously approached by a direct interview in which nothing is discussed but the child's difficulties. The interviewed parent will rarely acknowledge that the problem is due to alcoholism; almost never if the interview is with the alcoholic. Rarely will even the nonalcoholic parent admit it to a person felt to be a stranger; the protective instinct is very strong.

The interview works both ways, however, even if no mention is made of an alcoholic problem; the parent being interviewed will realize, perhaps for the first time, how seriously the child is being affected. This may be sufficient to cause the family to take positive action. But as a means of helping the child, the interview is an uncertain and long-range tool; the teacher is in a position to do something constructive for the child only in their daily meeting in class. The teacher can utilize the school regulations to create a sense of order and security, teach the child to meet problems realistically, and provide some of the training usually lacking at home. These efforts to help the child function in a normal manner may not be wholly successful, but with knowledge and compassion, the teacher can hope to make some improvement. In providing a measure of peace and stability, the child will be strengthened to withstand the damage of the alcoholic home. And the teacher who has had some contact with Al-Anon's principles will be all the better fortified for this task.

Those Who Live
With the Problem

The stories that follow were written by members of Al-Anon. They are the frankly-told experiences of people who have known deep trouble and who have tried to meet their difficulties with courage and honesty.

Those living with similar problems should find it helpful to know that many others have found answers—or at least a way to seek solutions.

SERENITY DOES NOT DEPEND ON SOBRIETY

When I see a newcomer at an Al-Anon meeting, with that typical look of fear and anxiety, my heart goes out to her. I want to tell her that serenity and peace of mind do not depend on her husband's sobriety. I would like to spare her the years of anguish I lived through before I learned that my serenity depends only on me.

For the first eighteen years of my marriage, my constant prayer was for my husband to stop drinking. At that time I had not heard of AA and didn't know what an alcoholic was!

My husband has been in and out of AA for the past several years, but only because of my pushing and threatening. He went to meetings only to appease me and not to help himself. I felt a constant weight of guilt. Was I to blame? What was my responsibility in this situation? I had to do something, I told myself; I must pray harder, go to church oftener. Should I leave him? Should I do this or that? I turned from one desperate solution to another.

With all this going through my mind, all I could think of was sleep—retreat from my problems. They were too overpowering. And I did sleep, by my own choice. I tried to take my life. When I woke up in the hospital my first thought was: God in Heaven, what have I done? What have I done to my children, my family—what fear have I put them through!

I owe my life to the help of Al-Anon and AA friends, to our priest (who is a good friend), to understanding doctors and to my wonderful and dear family. They were the instruments God used to pull me back from the depths of despair. The gift of life I received I compare to the gift the alcoholic receives when he finds his sobriety. My gratitude helped me to make peace with myself.

Through Al-Anon, after many years, I finally found my release. I took the first of our Twelve Steps, the one which says: "Admitted that we were powerless over alcohol, that our lives had become unmanageable." Now I accept the fact that I am powerless. I take care of myself and try to improve myself for my children, my family and for me. For the first time in years, I have begun to find happiness in little things. In the past I was too miserable to see things that were there all the time to be appreciated: each day has something good; the sun is shining, or it's raining and we needed rain; my children are well and happy.

Al-Anon is as necessary to me as the food I eat and the air I breathe. It is a wonderful help in facing all problems. They may be small or large—problems that go along with bringing up children, perhaps an illness, the loss of a loved one, or even a great crisis. I try to remember that out of every difficulty, every failure, some good will come. Perhaps not at once, perhaps as a guidepost to the handling of future difficulties.

I often think that for us God may have some special purpose. Many who have tried to help my husband have become stronger themselves when they have seen what he has gone through. So even in his way, unknowingly, he has helped someone else. Perhaps God's wish for me is to help other wives and families.

Thoughts of this kind are a great comfort to me. I no longer feel I'm deprived when I miss this party or that outing, when I can't go here or there. I consider what I have: my home, my four lovely children; I consider how much better off I am than my husband. He is the one who is missing so much, not I.

I must fulfill the role I was intended for: a wife, a mother, a member of society. I cannot do it as a self-pitying neurotic. I know that we are not sent more suffering than we can bear. This thought gives me strength for whatever may come.

When I first came to Al-Anon I didn't know what to expect. I had the attitude: I'm here, help me! I thought I would find an overnight solution to all my problems, but I found that Al-Anon's purpose is to show us how to help ourselves. Active participation in meetings, and plenty of reading, help things fall into place. Each day things become more clear to me.

There are blue days, of course. When they come, I say to myself: You have no time for self-pity. At such times I have to force myself to keep my mind off my troubles. The best therapy I have found is to keep busy. I take my house apart and clean and clean. I lose myself in a good novel. I have my hair done. I buy material and sew. And I've learned never to do things "with a vengeance." I just take them easy and savor every moment of accomplishing something.

I do not look on our problem as a cross to bear but as something that has been sent to show me a beautiful new way of life I would not have known otherwise. I have grown more aware of people; I have an urgent desire to help them find the kind of serenity I live with today. It has made me grateful for little things I used to take for granted—the sun, the trees, God's creatures and friends. I am trying to pass this way of living on to my children so they will know how to face problems with courage.

My greatest compliment came from my 14-year-old when he said to me: "Mom, how come you're so happy and dad is still drinking?"

Finally, my prayer is no longer: "Please, God, may it be Your will that my husband stops drinking," Now it is: "Please, God, show me Your way and give me the wisdom and strength to follow it."

Perhaps that's the answer.

LIVING WITH AL-ANON, WE LEARN TO LIVE

I am what is known as an old-timer, one who started to learn the AA program before Al-Anon was born. Though I have had many years of this good life, I still feel the need to attend meetings and to keep active by working with people. We progress in this program for as long as we live.

My husband drank for 25 years. Finally his drinking was completely out of control; it was heartbreaking to watch him disintegrating before my very eyes. During the last ten years he was a periodic drinker. When he was sober, I would tell myself, "This is the time. Now everything is going to be all right"—only to be plunged again into the depths of despair. I made all the mistakes that are so familiar to the wives of alcoholics, pouring liquor away, hiding the car keys, pleading and weeping to keep him from going out for more liquor. Nothing worked, yet I kept on repeating my mistakes.

Finally, recognizing my own irrational thinking, I was forced into a decision. I had many times threatened to leave him, but had never had the strength of purpose to follow through. I had been raised by strict parents who did all my thinking for me, and I was terrified at the thought of going out on my own. But it's amazing what you can do when you are finally desperate

enough. I enrolled in a business school and started divorce pro-
ceedings. Not long after this, my husband finally accepted AA.

I went to AA meetings with my husband and loved it. I attended the wives' group, as it was then called, but heard so
many complaints about the drinking husbands that I found no
help there. Six years later, Al-Anon came into being, and we
started a group in our home. Looking back, I can see that I was
adept at telling everyone else how to live, but was doing very little about improving my own thinking.

The first thing I really learned was that I must bring myself to
release my husband and my children from my direction and
domination. I believe my husband released me in this way from
the very day he joined AA. This meant I must keep hands off
his life and allow him to find his own answers in his own way,
even allowing him the freedom to make his own mistakes
without reproach or criticism from me. The second important
thing I learned was to release myself from the need for his approval and fear of his disapproval. I do what I do for free, with
no strings attached; I have to be myself, and do the best I can
with what I have.

I have learned to live by the Twelve Steps. The Fourth suggests an inventory of ourselves, and this is certainly of vital importance. There is some danger, however, of concentrating too
much on digging for defects of character.

Perhaps it would be more constructive to regard our defects
as character traits channeled in the wrong direction. Everyone
is born with a package of characteristics which remain pretty
much the same throughout life. I found that working the
Twelve Steps helped me to rechannel those traits into constructive, rather that destructive, attitudes.

Such faults as a tendency to self-pity, possessiveness, resentment and fear, for example, can be rechanneled into attitudes motivated by love. I had great pride—false pride, much of it. How could that be channeled into something constructive? Pride can be transformed into human dignity, which is pride plus humility, instead of selfishness. Although I was able to release people with love, I had failed to allow them the personal dignity which is the right of every human being. I am still learning to channel an excessive sensitivity into compassion and understanding.

I know the value of becoming more flexible. Unless we can bend with the wind, we're in trouble. I'm also trying to get rid of habitual "expectancy"—expecting others to perform the way I think they should, expecting things to happen in the way I think they should. This only creates frustration and disappointment.

During my husband's drinking years, I had completely lost my sense of humor, and even after I'd been in Al-Anon for years, I still couldn't find anything amusing about anything that had happened in the past. When we began talking about the value of the "light touch," I began to see what had happened to me. Instead of looking at my past mistakes with a bit of amused tolerance, I solemnly remembered only what a "stupid no-good" I'd been. The light touch helps avert many a family crisis in dealing with the alcoholic. When criticism and bitterness put the drinker on the defensive, a good natured flexibility avoids arousing hostility, and saves us from the emotional storms that tear us apart and solve nothing.

For many years now, my husband and I have been following the same path, like the two rails of a single track, separately, yet together. I am sorry for families who have not taken refuge in the Al-Anon program and especially for those who object to their mates' attending AA meetings. When an alcoholic finds this way of life, he often grows so fast that we must learn to grow with him or the relationship may be in danger. For this is a family disease. It needs a family answer. In order to achieve real unity, the whole family needs to practice the AA and Al-Anon principles, each in his individual way.

PERFECTLY GOOD PEOPLE GET ALCOHOLISM: A PROFESSIONAL LOOKS AT HER ATTITUDES

I don't know what made me look for a job in an alcoholic treatment unit when I graduated from nursing school. Maybe it was God guiding me. Anyway, there I was—up to my enema bags in drunks. As part of my responsibilities I had to attend a weekly Al-Anon meeting.

When I was a teenager, a friend invited me to attend Alateen with her because I was complaining about my alcoholic father. I declined. I thought I didn't need help from anyone. I knew all there was to know about getting by in an alcoholic family. That was still the song I was singing as I prepared to attend my first Al-Anon meeting!

I thought I knew what Al-Anon was about. It was the place where people got together to talk about how awful it is to be stuck with an alcoholic. It also served to get them out of the house for a few hours without feeling guilty. In that sense, I was happy to attend Al-Anon: the opportunity to get away from the nursing floor was very appealing. But I was about to find out how wrong I was about Al-Anon!

The hospital-based meeting was held in the patients' lounge of the alcoholic treatment unit. The Al-Anon Institutions group was designed to introduce the patients' family members to Al-

Anon. I recognized some of the people in the room as spouses of my patients. They looked a little jumpy and a lot depressed. I remember wanting to ask them: "What keeps you tied to an alcoholic? Do you love him that much? Are you crazy? Do you enjoy being a sad-sack? Why don't you get out?"

I'm glad no one was able to read my mind, to hear my cruel questions. There were other people in the room, too, who didn't look jumpy or depressed. As I watched, they chatted and seemed relaxed, even cheerful, although to my mind they did seem a little smug. I was curious about who they were.

As I sat there wondering, a man walked in. The chatting stopped and all eyes turned to watch as he sat down and started to arrange pamphlets in neat stacks in front of him. I guessed, correctly, that our leader had arrived. He introduced himself as Bill and began to tell us about how he used to react to his qualifier's drinking. Then he told us about what Al-Anon had taught him and how his reactions to the drinking had changed. He described how changes in his behavior had allowed the alcoholic the freedom to become sober. I could feel myself becoming defensive. I had tried everything I could to get my own dad sober, and nothing had worked. Now this man was telling us that the alcoholic is the one who needs to be given freedom? It seemed to me that the drunk is the only one who does what he pleases and everyone around him is trapped. It never occurred to me that my dad might have been trapped, too.

I left that meeting a little irritated. I wasn't sure why. Was it the sad-sack spouses? Or the bright-eyed "know it all" members? Or was the irritation caused by old conflicts coming back to haunt me? Was I still, after all these years, a sad-sack, too? I was glad to get out of that meeting and back to work.

Sooner than I liked, I had to attend the Al-Anon meeting again. It started in the same way as the first, with Bill leading the meeting. I was only half listening when all of a sudden a charge of electricity shot through me and I sat bolt upright. It was a statement Bill made. He said, "Perfectly good people get the perfectly dreadful disease of alcoholism." My response was immediate and intense. I heard myself say out loud, "If good people can get it, so can perfectly dreadful people." I was embarrassed at the hostility in my voice. I was also surprised that my comment didn't bring about a hostile reply. My group suggested, in a caring way, that I had not yet accepted alcoholism as a disease and that when I did, I would feel differently.

I thought that over for a while. What was going on here? If I embraced the disease concept of alcoholism, I'd have to stop hating my dad. How could I give that up? It was such a perfect defense against feeling hurt. I spent a good deal of time thinking about my attitudes and how they were interfering with my growth not only as a person but also as a professional working with alcoholics. I talked to friends and co-workers about my problem. They agreed I needed to work on this area of my life. By the time I attended my third hospital-based Al-Anon meeting, I had made up my mind to attend other meetings outside the hospital.

I'm beginning to see peace of mind in Al-Anon members where I once saw smugness. I want some peace of mind myself. These members say they get it from Al-Anon. Maybe I can, too.

THE FACE OF AN ANGEL

My daughter has the face of an angel. She is an adult who has always earned a great deal of money through her modeling. Sometimes, I could just cry out when I look at her because she seems so perfect. But I ask myself, "What is going to happen to that face when her drinking really begins to show?" Oh, I know her looks will suffer—I've had my own experience with the havoc alcohol can play with one's body; but the loss of beauty is really the least of my concerns. I'm afraid for her.

I'm also angry. I thought that having gone through her early childhood as the daughter of an alcoholic (me), she would have known better than to do what I did. And I feel guilty. I wonder all the time if *my* drinking caused *her* drinking.

It was my long-time Al-Anon wife who suggested that there was help for me in her program. At first, as a member of AA, I resisted. After all, I had a program of recovery of my own, and I used it to keep myself sober. What did I have to learn in Al-Anon?

But I *am* learning. I am learning how to let go of my daughter and her behavior. I am resisting the temptation to find solutions for the trouble she has caused by her drinking. Every day I am trying not to prolong her illness by paying her bills, or covering up for her drinking behavior. The last time she was pulled over by the highway patrol, I did not offer to pay her fine, nor put up her bail money.

I focus on the part I play in her life as her father, guided by the mothers and fathers, brothers and sisters and children of alcoholics I find in Al-Anon. I think I am experiencing a totally new attitude by learning to let go of my children, to surrender to a Higher Power who I believe watches over me and will watch over them. But it is a very hard thing to do, and I believe I couldn't do it without the help and understanding given me by my Al-Anon friends. So I try, just one day at a time, to trust that God will take care of my daughter, and I will let go and let him.

DETACHMENT AS ONE GRANDFATHER SEES IT

My grown son was in trouble. I had not known about the drinking because he had been away in the army. But when he returned I could see how alcohol had ravaged his mind, and I was devastated. The boy I had watched grow into a man had disappeared, leaving an angry, despondent stranger in his place.

My desolation was made complete when I went to visit my three grandchildren. They were in terrible straits, their abandonment almost certain because their mother was drinking, too. Once I got on the plane home, I cried for the entire trip, despite my age. As often as I could, I returned to that horrible scene to cook a decent meal, take a grandchild to the park, or help another struggle through a school assignment. My wife would move through the household clutter, washing clothes, cleaning the week's dishes and taking out the accumulated garbage. Then those terrible flights home were always waiting for us.

"Get off my back," my son had said over and over again. "Just get off my back," and heaven only knows I wished I could. There seemed no answers to any of our problems until I found Al-Anon. The loving concern for me and my family was apparent from the start. People understood my anguish, and in a caring way helped me to see that my kind of caring wasn't helping me, my wife, my son or his family. They helped me to understand that I would have to learn a new way to help, one that might take considerable knowledge of myself.

Detachment seemed a last resort because at first sight it appeared to be unhelpful. Yet detachment can be a very misunderstood word. I soon learned that it is a description of a very positive principle. With detachment, I could separate myself from my son and daughter-in-law's illness—from their addiction and compulsion—without cutting myself off from them as people I loved. With detachment, I could give them over to a Higher Power, one I had come to know and love myself.

These are the things I began to believe: I must look to my own well-being and serenity, to the exclusion of all else—spouse, family, job, whatever. If I did not, then all these things would be of no consequence. Put bluntly, if I could not save anything or anyone else, I would have to save myself. Detachment did not mean disinterest; that would express only despair and hopelessness. No, I considered detachment "respect for another's personhood." With detachment I learned that:

> I must not become involved emotionally with the results of the illness.
> I cannot make anyone do or act as I think, unless he or she wants to.
> I must keep an open mind and a closed mouth to learn to change my attitudes.
> I must stop participating in the "games" that no one wins.
> I must learn to give those I love the right to make their own mistakes and recognize them as theirs alone.

I could accept the problems that confronted me and try to handle them with understanding and courage, through the help of Al-Anon and a Higher Power. I was able to recognize that I was to blame for many situations and learn to "let go."

With this tool I was able to keep hands off my family's situation and not interfere while my son found his own way to recovery. And it worked: without me, he saw the results of his drinking in his home and with his children. When he saw what was happening, he couldn't face the situation and asked for help in AA.

I still go to Al-Anon. My grandchildren's mother continues to drink, and I often struggle with the old emotions after they visit me. I know what they are going home to, and I still hurt thinking about it. The difference today is that I have Al-Anon to deal with my reality and to help me decide what I can or should do, without the old attitude of hopelessness. I have put some money in trust for my granddaughter's education. I call and write regularly to show that I love them unconditionally. Oh, I know they can melt me with their bright eyes, but I am trying not to be manipulated by their situation. Their father is sober and they have some Alateen meetings under their belts, although sometimes their mother won't let them go. My son has the wisdom to tell me not to repeat my old ways and to let his children discover their own realities and learn how to grow up in them. And I have my Al-Anon fellowship, my friends and my program to keep reminding me.

"LET GO AND LET GOD"—
A DEEPENING SENSE OF
DETACHMENT HELPS A SON

In taking a close look at the way I act, I have come to realize how important it is for me to learn to love unconditionally. As an Al-Anon member, I must steer a steady course between the twin defects of strong dislike on the one hand and suffocating closeness on the other. With practice, I have come to grasp what is meant by loving and letting go. This principle sums up for me what I conceive detachment to be.

When I first came into Al-Anon, I had long ago given up any pretense at serenity, for my life was truly unmanageable. My son was an active alcoholic; one of my daughters was living with a similarly addicted person, and another was trying to cope with an autistic child. My wife had come from an alcoholic background, and I was recovering from the effects of a serious auto accident.

My understanding of the principle of detachment was at first rudimentary. I learned that I could indeed walk away from alcoholic behavior that was in any way irrational or harassing. I learned to be "a target out of range," so to speak. This physical detachment offered me a temporary calm in which I could get my thinking straight. But I have to admit that it did not help

107

me with the feelings of resentment and apprehension these occurrences were apt to stir up within me.

Gaining strength in Al-Anon, I learned that I did not have to leave the scene in order to find a sense of serenity. More importantly, I was no longer accepting the burden of guilt which the alcoholic and other family members had been able to place handily on my shoulders. It was interesting that, at this stage, I felt free to pursue my own interests, both inside and outside the home. I became happily busy in new, creative endeavors.

As my sense of detachment deepened, I felt my attitude toward the Al-Anon program begin to change. At first, meetings had been like a ready-made escape hatch whenever the going got rough at home. Now I felt that my Higher Power was blessing me with a new family in Al-Anon, and my sense of unconditional love became stronger as I came to realize that members of my own family were entitled to be regarded as in every way worthy of God-given dignity and respect—especially those who had unfortunately been afflicted with the disease of alcoholism. Continued involvement in the Al-Anon program, its love, understanding and support was helping to dissolve my resentments, fears and self-pity. I began to realize that I could place this family of mine in the hands of a Higher Power who really loved them and go about my business with an increasing sense of tranquillity and self-esteem.

I believe that my own growth in the Al-Anon program and my understanding of the principles of detachment were eventually helpful to my alcoholic son. When circumstances warranted invoking the Order of Protection I had been granted by the Family Court, my son was offered by the Court the choice of treatment, incarceration or voluntarily leaving my home. He chose the latter course. Now that he has taken some steps toward responsibility for himself, I feel I must free him *completely,* and let him go. Detaching with love and the continuing help of the Al-Anon program has helped improve our relationship in a way that is advantageous to both of us.

A NEWCOMER TO AL-ANON
SEARCHES FOR IDENTITY

Right after I turned fourteen, my father died unex-
pectedly, and from that time on, my mother began drinking
very heavily. It seemed that overnight I went from childhood to
adulthood with no adolescence in between. There was one saving grace; during high school, I began to make some very close
friends, which I still have today. Yet I was not able to invite
friends over to my house, for fear of my mother's growing use of
violence and verbal abuse. I remember thinking that bad things
really *could* happen to me. In fact, they *were* happening to me
because they *should* happen to me. Then I took my reasoning a
step too far: unconsciously, I assigned myself a life of sadness
that became a self-fulfilling prophecy.

I left home when I went to college and never really returned,
except for vacations. I was very cautious in my relationships
with the opposite sex. Nevertheless, at nineteen I fell madly in
love. I threw my entire being into the relationship and, when it
didn't work out, I was crushed. My self-esteem hit rock bottom
and stayed there for some time.

In college I became a hippie. I discovered "grass" and continued to smoke it every day for the next 12 years. I was never
interested in alcohol, however; visions of my mother prevented

that. It felt good to be a part of a group that, like me, didn't fit in with the rest of society. I majored in art. My abilities were growing, and after graduation I felt free to search for my identity anywhere except in the city where my mother lived. I came to New York because I felt it was the center for artistic expression.

About this time, my mother's boyfriend accused me of being the most miserable person he had ever met. I was shocked. I didn't even know I was miserable, because I didn't know what happiness was. What I did know about was sadness, hurt and loneliness.

Soon after I arrived in New York, I met someone whom I could love. We married eight months later. He was an alcoholic who needed a nurse and a mother. Well, so did I. We stayed married for four years, at which point I picked a fight with him. When he swung at me, I left him. I didn't dare go back because it took me two years to stand up for myself. After three years neither of us has had the courage to seek a divorce. Although I sought help from a psychologist during my marriage, it didn't help much because I didn't look at my problems from the point of view of alcohol abuse and its effects.

Six months ago, I made a decision to get the help I needed. I began going to Al-Anon. This has meant that I have had to stop leaning emotionally on my friends who, though sympathetic, could not help me. In Al-Anon, I am learning that other children of alcoholics have had the same problems I have had, and have been helped. I was able to identify with Al-Anon members because we have all had the same kinds of feelings and have taken the same wrong turns in our attempts to find solutions to life's problems. I am learning not to take my disappointments out on myself by overeating, smoking grass and overworking. I still don't trust people in intimate situations, although I do keep my long-term friendships and I am beginning to make some new ones in Al-Anon.

Sometimes, as I struggle to recover from the effects of my mother's and husband's alcoholism, I still feel like the original "bad luck kid"—the role I assigned myself when my father died and my mother began drinking. I am still more comfortable in "underdog" roles, rather than being successful, although now it helps to share this at Al-Anon meetings. I have lived for a long time intellectualizing my problems. I used to argue that, since no one was there to ask about my feelings, it was obvious no one cared. Now, with the help of the Al-Anon program, I feel that if I don't take care of myself, I will continue to suffer. There is a growing desire in me not to do that any longer. I don't really know how to go about it, but I do honestly believe that Al-Anon meetings, especially those attended by children of alcoholics, will provide me with the answers I seek. I only wish my brothers and sisters could get the help I am getting.

I can see now that all my problems will be better approached from a position of serenity, and I intend to try to achieve this state of being by attending Al-Anon meetings and no longer abusing myself. I hope to learn how to love myself, with the help of Al-Anon's Twelve Steps of Recovery. Perhaps the rest of the solutions will follow.

I BELONG TO SOMETHING

I grew up without parents. I do not mean to say I have no mother or father: I do. But both my parents were 18 years old when I was born, and they never learned to grow up.

My mother was the only daughter of a well-to-do Southern family, my father the son of a construction contractor. They eloped when they had known each other 13 days. Neither family ever quite forgave them. I did not know my mother's family until I was grown.

My father was a Martin. The Martins were not a family. We were a clan. There was one set of rules for the rest of the world to follow—and another set of rules for the Martins. Martins did not steal. Martins did not lie. Martins did not go into debt, and Martins did things better than anyone else. The slogan of my grandfather's business was "For A Better Job Call Martin and Sons."

I remember a remark made by my favorite aunt when she met my tall, good-looking husband. She watched him walk out of a room, so straight and broad-shouldered, smiled at me and said, "He will do nicely, my dear, when he has been 'Martinized.' " She was not referring to a recently-developed cleaning process and thank God, we were never successful in "Martinizing" Bill.

My father was the third son of his family and an alcoholic. Oh, we didn't call him an alcoholic. He was referred to as "that irresponsible Martin Boy," "the black sheep of of the family," and after Grandfather's death, "the town drunk."

Grandfather paid his way out of scrapes and bailed him out of jail. When Dad left a bridge half-built or a schoolhouse without a roof, Grandfather sent others to finish the job and nothing was said about it. The family felt sorry for "John's children," of course.

If I were to answer the question, "What is the most vivid remembrance of your childhood?" I'd have to say it was my father building a fence around the houses we occupied in various construction camps around the country. This fence was not to keep the Martin children in—it was to keep the other people *out*. We did not need people.

I never belonged anywhere. I never belonged in a school, a church, or a community. I never had a friend. I was a good student—I liked to read. In my story-book world, all the people were good and beautiful. I much preferred them to real people. I was graduated from high school at the top of my class and assumed I would go to college. This was expected of a Martin. When it was time for me to make arrangements for college entrance, however, my father told me there was no money. I knew he had drunk it up, and at that moment I hated my father. It took me many years to forgive him.

When I married, all the pride, all the loyalty and all the love I had never been able to express was lavished on my husband— and later on my children.

When drinking became a problem in our marriage, I refused to recognize it. As the disease progressed, I withdrew. I attempted to return to my story-book world but it did not work so well. I had to face reality and know the anguish that all of us know who watch someone we love sink into the abyss of alcoholism. I

watched this terrible compulsion all but destroy him. It took
away everything he wanted to keep.

Bill lost his left arm and his left eye as the result of drinking,
and he could not stop. He lost his self-respect and the confidence of his family as the result of drinking, and he could not
stop. He almost died as the result of drinking, *and he could not
stop.* I watched this happen and could do nothing to help him.
As Bill's drinking progressed, all the personality defects I had
brought to our marriage became greatly intensified. We became
two very sick people.

When I came to Al-Anon I was completely bankrupt in all
areas of living. I had no faith in God. Oh, I believed in a
Supreme Being, a Creator of the Universe who changed the
seasons, who made day into night and hung out the stars. But I
did not believe He could help me.

I know now that when I was frightened and cold—and sometimes angry—I tried to pray. I believe He heard me say, "Oh,
God," and knew I couldn't find the words that prayers were
made of. I believe He listens very closely for the prayers of
amateurs because He knows our great need and that we
sometimes do not have the courage to speak aloud.

I did not trust my fellow man. I could not even trust myself. I
was not responsible for the things I said or did. I could not cope
with the tensions of normal living. When it was important for
me to be calm. I went into hysterics. I was so impatient with our
four lovely children that they were afraid of me. I could not talk
to Bill—we had nothing to say.

When Bill finally did stop drinking, I had no confidence in
his sobriety. I did not believe AA would work. I hoped it would,
I wanted it to, but I didn't believe it would. I could not understand how a group of strangers who did not love Bill as I did

could possibly help him when I had failed—I who was a Martin, and not born to fail.

I attended the Al-Anon meetings and listened with tongue in cheek when the members spoke of daily prayer and meditation, and did not believe them. But I was intelligent enough to know that I must have this program to restore my mental health. So at first I started mechanically to apply the principles of the Al-Anon program to myself, and things began to change. No longer was I hysterical, unpredictable, as I had been for years. When I could begin to laugh at myself, I knew I was getting well. My children began to relax around me, and I knew my husband was proud of me.

What meant so much to me was the awareness that I belonged to something. I belonged to the most wonderful group of people in the world. I had hundreds of friends, and some of you said you liked me. So at last I joined the human race. I am no longer alone. I thank God for those of you who kept this program alive until I came along. I shall spend the rest of my life trying to pay my tremendous debt of gratitude to all of you, everywhere.

A "NOBODY" BECOMES A "SOMEBODY" THROUGH SERVICE IN AL-ANON

I came into Al-Anon seven years ago as a "nobody." I truly believed this because alcoholism, the family disease, had told me so on a daily basis for thirteen years. I attended a lot of meetings, got a sponsor, read the literature and meditated on a daily basis. I needed a lot of input to change my thinking toward the positive. I started to believe that as an Al-Anon member I was a "somebody," and that maybe, just maybe, I counted as a person.

I had a spiritual slip when I attended a state Convention with my husband, who is the alcoholic, and our daughter, whom we had been forcing to attend Alateen meetings. The first night there, she told us that she hated her dad for being an alcoholic and she wanted him to be "normal." I thought my heart would break, and once again I felt like a "nobody." But at that first Convention so many doors opened for us as a family. Our daughter started to identify with other Alateens and began to accept commitments in the Convention at round robin meetings and on Convention Committees, and I met Al-Anon members who were enhancing their recoveries through service.

Because I enjoyed their company, I began to just "hang out" at Al-Anon Convention planning meetings, and eventually I was asked to help. I heard my name being placed in nomination for

Al-Anon Chairman of a Convention. Later my husband was elected Chairman of the AA Convention. Still later that day, our daughter told us she had been elected Chairman for the Alateens. We all felt excited and loved, if a bit awed by our new responsibilities.

My husband, our daughter and I have all just "hung-out" one more year in Convention planning meetings. What a way to spend our weekends—with people who really care and know what to do with their spare time and want to be involved in something worthwhile! We are kinder to each other, too. It is hard to find time to take each other's inventories when all three of us are on our way to a program meeting.

Today, I'm a somebody in Al-Anon. Oh, I don't mean to sound as though getting an Al-Anon service job gave me some sort of position where I was the "boss" or the person in charge. Rather, having the job helped me change my selfishness into giving. I now truly know how it feels when someone quotes from our Second Tradition: "Our leaders are but trusted servants." Other Al-Anons walked beside me all year to give their best in helping put together their Convention. I have found out that the finest members are involved in all levels of service, where they can enjoy everyone's recovery. They know that service doesn't make you a big deal—it's part of what's happening, it's *giving*.

Al-Anon Conventions have taught me just to *begin* to live. On the morning after the Convention this year I received a phone call telling me that my sponsor's husband had had a heart attack. I spent three days with her and her family, giving back some of the support she had so unselfishly given me over the past year. You see, I got out of myself and got into doing the work in this program of being there for somebody else. So there was no need to be a "nobody" anymore.

I know a family can recover together, sharing what they were given through service to others in their program. It doesn't matter if we feel inadequate to the job we are given, for others in our fellowship will walk with us. I know that all I had to do was just show up, and I became a "somebody" again.

ON EXAMINING ONE'S OWN FAULTS

Step Four of the Twelve Steps on which our program is based says: "Made a searching and fearless moral inventory of ourselves."

When I came into Al-Anon some years ago, I knew I *wanted* help, but not until I had been attending Al-Anon for a while did I realize how much help I *needed*.

The first six years of my marriage were spent in an alcoholic whirlpool with life going around in dizzying circles. Alcohol seemed to pull down everything and everyone it touched until the future looked dark indeed. Along came the miracle of AA, and the last six years of marriage have included sobriety. Should this suddenly disappear, I would still be grateful for the opportunity I have had for comparison. Yet I must face the fact that it will still take much soul-searching to improve the amount of communication and cooperation and to lessen tension and crises. The one obviously upsetting ingredient has been removed. What's the answer to further improvement?

For a long time I have been adept at taking my mate's inventory—at the drop of a promise or the notice of an unpaid bill. Strangely enough, this has not made me expert at taking my own! I have discovered how difficult it is to take an objective look at myself. And I would strongly recommend trying it, even to those who are new in Al-Anon. What an inventory reveals may not be tranquilizing, but there is good sense in turning the spotlight on yourself.

The alcoholic has succeeded in convincing you that your nagging and your outlandish demands make him so miserable that he must drink to endure it. Society says your home is different—the atmosphere is not a good one in which to rear children. Once we're indoctrinated with these ideas, we decide we aren't worth much.

An honest personal inventory will help dispel this illusion. We will realize that we are individuals with distinct personalities which an inventory will define—the good and the bad.

In our eagerness to be fair and honest, we usually go overboard in the beginning; the list of undesirable traits far outweighs the good ones. Our feelings of guilt, which may or may not be justified, should not be allowed to distort the picture. As we grow in Al-Anon "know-how," we acquire a sharper awareness, and the qualities we list in our inventories change as we go along and learn. For this reason, Step Four, like the other eleven, must be taken over and over again.

Looking back over my six years in Al-Anon, I am particularly impressed with the factor of change. This includes everything from my interpretation of the various Steps to the practical application I make of the program. It certainly includes my attitude with regard to the items found in my inventory. I used to be ashamed that I didn't have Janet's faith, or Jill's patience, or Louise's lack of resentment. Now I am more realistic. Unless I should suddenly be elevated to sainthood, there will always be items on both sides of the list. I am confident that with the help of my Higher Power I can develop some of the better qualities and erase less desirable ones.

On the other hand, character defects are a human weakness,

and my frustration is diminished if I keep in mind that I will not attain perfection in this life. For example, I am no longer embarrassed that I occasionally experience self-pity. I recognize it a lot sooner than I used to, and I usually can put my finger on the cause. Above all, I try to take measures to get rid of it. Though Al-Anon is an excellent guide for living, its effectiveness depends upon the action of the individual. To discover what areas need attention and improvement, it is essential to take inventory of ourselves.

Getting back to the wording of the Fourth Step, we find "fearless." If there is one emotion associated with the illness of alcoholism, it is fear. We have lived with it, slept and wept with it. For this reason, the suggestion that we be *fearless* assumes real significance. In examining my own feelings about the terrible fear I felt in the past, I decided it was fed by my ignorance and wavering faith. We are apt to be frightened by things we do not understand and over which we cannot gain control. Alcoholism and the alcoholic certainly fall into this category, but the Al-Anon program provides us with knowledge to replace this fear. It also reminds us, in Step Three, to turn our lives over to the care of God, as we understand Him. Like oil and water, fear and faith just don't mix.

An inventory is a very personal undertaking, and a difficult one, but so is life, even when we are facing it just 24 hours at a time. Relying on our Higher Power and the Twelve Steps of Al-Anon gives us support and direction for our days.

OUT OF THE FOG—INTO THE CLEAR

This morning, on our way to work, our travel was hampered by fog. It wasn't the fleeting thick-and-thin kind, but a heavy white blanket that shut out everything within a few feet of the car. Familiar road signs and landmarks were so obscured that it was difficult to know where to make the next turn.

In the same way, blanketings of fog can settle over us in our daily lives—fogs of confusion, uncertainty, discouragement. Even after many years of diligently applying Al-Anon teachings, we may become helpless and lost about the next turn to take.

This incident happened to me:

One day I had a sudden impulse to telephone one of my Al-Anon friends. As I spoke to her and listened to her response, I realized that she had somehow become enveloped in a fog. She had let go of the wonderful hope and faith she had gained through working with the Al-Anon program for more than a year. Her despair left me stunned. My words of encouragement seemed to fall away into space before they could reach her. I felt helpless, and almost as hopeless, as she sounded.

How could I make her understand that we, in Al-Anon, are not guaranteed a free and easy climb to complete serenity? Most of us will have times when we will fall back into old habits and despairs, times when those on the sidelines can only look on and pray that we will again let God show us the way we seem to have lost in a blinding mental fog.

My fog has cleared. I know I must accept this: we cannot save everyone from anxiety and despair. We of Al-Anon can help only those who accept this philosophy and who will hang on to it, come what may.

And then, with my own fogged thinking cleared, came a letter from my friend. My telephone call, she says, must have been an act of God. It changed her pattern of thinking, and she is back on the Al-Anon road again. For a time she can see the road ahead. If anxiety and doubt should again fog her vision, she has my continued prayers that her way will soon loom up again bright and clear.

A RETURN TO FAITH
BY WAY OF AL-ANON

I was a spoiled, only child. I had seven grandparents and great-grandparents whom I learned early to manipulate and control. It was not until I met alcohol (not that which I drank, but that drunk by my husband) that I found something I could not control.

I had been brought up to worship God. I had no idea it was not *worship* He wanted, but for us to *live* His way 24 hours a day. I did not know that He knew we were too weak to do this alone, and was happy to do it for us...if we *asked* Him.

I had become an agnostic, and I had to find out what chaos could result from managing my own life before I was ready to give my precious "me" to Him to manage. I am forever grateful that being married to an alcoholic did this for me. Some have much worse troubles. Some never have the troubles they need to find this.

Why *I* am not an alcoholic can only be by the Grace of God, perhaps because of some chemical balance He has given my body. I started drinking at the age of 10 when my girl friend and I tapped her father's whiskey. I continued in boarding school and college. I drank with my husband.

Why, as he drank more, I began to drink less, I have no idea. We have much the same personality. Our differences are these: I have an inborn caution; he has not. I am not a perfectionist;

he is. He had alcoholics in his family; I had only neurotics whom I followed with emotional gusto.

I do not remember finding his drinking a problem until after our son was born. My husband was jealous of my affection for our child. I do remember my first truly humiliating encounter with my powerlessness over it, one winter night when he was home on leave during World War II. I helped him home from a dance, telephone pole by telephone pole, up Main Street, a mile or more. As a finale, in frustrated fury, I kicked his prostrate frame at the foot of the last pole. The next Saturday he was righteously indignant when I dragged a toboggan from the stable to facilitate bringing him home from the dance!

There is no use describing the wailings and gnashings of teeth, the businesses lost, the jobs quit before he was fired. Suffice it to say that the Korean War came along, and he escaped into the Air Force.

Through a Guiding Hand he met a congenial drinking companion on a slip from AA. They were nearly court-martialed together in Korea. My husband escaped as he always seemed to. His friend Fred lost rank.

A couple of years later they found themselves stationed together again, this time with families in tow. Fred was back in AA—to my husband's amusement. But when he got into a drinking scrape he went to Fred, who lent him money he couldn't afford. He also suggested AA, and out of gratitude my husband attended a few meetings.

Fred's wife, Mary, became my private Al-Anon tutor. For the first time, although I had always thought I was fairly intelligent, I realized exactly what sort of problem we faced. A disease! Not stubbornness, irresponsibility, unkindness, selfishness, or temper—but a disease!

I had many of the same defects, *without* the disease! Mary's Al-Anon support and reading AA and Al-Anon literature helped me to learn to extend myself for others, even if only a little.

We were sent to another station, and after another fright, my husband signed the "pledge" for a year. It was wonderful. Our life suddenly began to emerge from its murk. We did things together. I found he could carry on an intelligent conversation in groups or at home. I became complacent.

Then he was sent to Thule, Greenland. My son and I went home. Still, things were fine. I had a sober husband, although at a distance. I had a car to drive when I wanted. I attended church smugly and regularly. I was profound in a "great books" group, athletic and social with golf and bowling. I actually remember wondering how people could think life was *hard!*

I met my husband at a hotel a hundred miles from home on his return from Greenland. The first thing he did was order a cocktail! I had needed my complacency clobbered, and it was. I went into an emotional tailspin as close to a nervous breakdown as I ever want to be. I forgot all the Al-Anon I had ever learned.

Lo and behold! Who should be out of the service and living near our new station? Fred and Mary! She began to get me back on the beam. I was desperate enough by now to try anything. I tried saying, "You take me, God, and run me. I can't."

No miracles occurred. It's like doing daily calisthenics. It's only after you've been practicing them a long time that results begin to show.

At first you have to keep giving yourself and your fears and your self-pity back to God, trusting Him to take them and work out your problems *through you*—by showing you what to do, and when to do it. After a while you begin to realize that He is doing just that, and you gradually learn to put *all* your affairs in His hands, *leaving* them there, *refusing* to doubt. Each time it becomes easier. You find it works with any problem, from messed-up plumbing to fighting city hall, from what to wear to a certain affair to an alcoholic husband. You can go to bed and serenely to sleep, and leave him, and even those his drinking may injure, to God.

At first this attitude angered my husband. I didn't *love* him! I wasn't *worried* about him! But seven years after his first encounter with AA, following a four-day disappearance, he went back to AA. I had had no idea where he was, but I didn't panic. I just kept asking God to help him wherever he was, and thrusting my worry away when it tried to creep back.

For five years, with the help of AA and Al-Anon, we have been growing together, both in the maturing sense and in the things we do and enjoy. It took 20 years, but our new marriage is worth it. It's not always smooth. We often have to hand over to God the things about our partner that bother us, along with our own. But we know with this Friend to guide us, we don't have to worry as long as we listen, and obey, and say "Thanks."

Giving yourself and your affairs to Him in complete surrender and absolute trust *works*. We don't *need* to know *why*.

SPIRITUAL AWAKENING

In Al-Anon I have come to understand what is meant by a "spiritual awakening" as a part of recovery. My experience, as a result of practicing the Twelve Steps, that a power greater than myself is guiding my life, is quite dramatic.

It was a very cold, windy and icy day in early January. My husband and I had made a commitment to attend an AA function in an institution near Kingston, Ontario, and we were planning to go no matter what the weather. We started out very early Saturday morning on our usual three-hour trip, but that day, as we headed east, the forecast was for extremely hazardous conditions.

We came upon more and more cars in the ditch or off the road. There were people walking to service stations, but we pressed on. Usually a two-lane highway, the road was now only open to one lane, and even that was tough going. We were careful, but moved along nonetheless.

As we rounded a slight curve, we suddenly came upon stalled cars in the middle of this one lane, but we could not stop! My heart was in my mouth. We whooshed past these cars and headed over the edge of the road toward a deep, snow-filled ditch with telephone poles at the bottom.

My husband had had driving experience in some of the worst road conditions in Canada, but even he was slightly panic-stricken because he yelled, "We'll be all right as long as it doesn't flip!"

Now we were going full force down the embankment, sideways. I was so afraid that I reached over to grab my husband's arm for comfort. Then, a thought came suddenly into my head so loudly that I couldn't believe where it was coming from.

The thought told me to free his arm. If he was to keep the car in control, he would have to have room to do it. I took my hand away, sat back straight in my bucket seat and waited for what I surely thought would be the end. We went down into the ditch, then back up the other side onto the road again, facing the direction in which we had been headed, with the motor still running!

We drove a half mile or so down the highway to a roadside gas station, where we checked the damage to the car and ourselves. When the hood was raised, it was packed with snow—and that car used to stall out in rain puddles! This time, it was still running.

My husband and I talked about our feelings and thoughts during the ordeal, and we both came to the conclusion that our Higher Power didn't want us to drive any further. We turned toward home. That was one of the most peaceful and pleasant drives we have ever had. The sun was shining, the ice was melting and the sky was clear of clouds. Just unbelievable! We think about that day often, and I feel it was a "spiritual awakening" because I know my Higher Power was guiding me then and is still, through unmistakably clear and strong thoughts—thoughts that I know aren't of *my* making!

A LATE-COMER INTO AL-ANON
FINDS SERENITY

I am a senior citizen and a great-grandmother, but I needed the Al-Anon program many, many years ago. I was born and raised in an alcoholic home. In those days one did not talk openly about alcoholism: it was kept a deep, dark secret. Alcoholics Anonymous had not yet come into being.

Remembering our family situation, I can see why I had so many living problems. Although we didn't have a name for it then, my father was the alcoholic. I was the oldest of eight children, so at an early age I had to work hard on the farm. My father was a very exacting man: nothing we did ever seemed to please him. We were all terrified at his outbursts of anger because he often became violent with us and our mother. I grew up with a sense of insecurity and a lack of self-worth. To add to my problems, I also suffered a severe loss of hearing early in life, because of physical abuse, and this continued to be a handicap to me for most of my life. My education was sketchy because of absenteeism for farm work and because I was constantly changing schools. We moved our residence every three or four months.

As I grew up, I was determined that, if I were to marry, it would be to a man who did not drink and who could give me a home with some stability. Well, suffice it to say I *did* marry a man who did not drink and did not move about. Nonetheless, the marriage ended in divorce. I felt I was a failure even in marriage. I had three lovely children, but in the daily struggle to make ends meet, I found little time to enjoy them.

Twenty years later I married my present husband. We were together only a short time when I discovered, much to my consternation, that he had a problem with drinking. However, being in a state of denial, I refused to recognize it as alcoholism: after all, I had promised myself that I was never going to marry an alcoholic!

As his disease grew worse, I also became ill and quite distraught from loss of sleep and lack of appetite. Not only was I physically debilitated but mentally impaired as well. One morning I decided that life was no longer worth living. I put on my coat, leaving the house in disarray from the night before, and walked, crying all the way, to a busy city intersection, determined to walk into the traffic and end my life.

Then, as I stepped off the curb, something—or someone—made me turn back. Weeping the whole way, I arrived home to find a neighbor at my door. I reluctantly invited her in. She could not help seeing the glasses, empty bottles and overflowing ashtrays. She must also have noticed my red and swollen eyes, for she asked me point-blank if I was living with the problem of alcoholism. I could not longer cover up or deny it, so I confessed that I was. Needless to say, it was through that dear lady that I was led to Al-Anon.

Today, I am still living with my husband of thirteen years, who remains an active alcoholic. But through this beautiful program of Al-Anon and the love and caring of the people in it, my life has changed. Although I arrived late in life, I have discovered that it is possible to find serenity at any age. My recovery was accomplished by using the Twelve Steps of the Al-Anon program and allowing God to take over my life. Through Al-Anon I found the courage to get a hearing aid. My hearing is not perfect, of course, but so much better that I now can do things I never thought possible.

Some years ago I was able to tell my father how I felt—that I loved him and, more importantly, that I forgave him. By then he was an old man, and I did not want him to go to his grave with my miserable, unforgiving spirit of so many years. Just a little over a year ago, while I was in the hospital for major surgery, my father died and I was unable to go to his funeral. But I was at peace with myself. Had I not known Al-Anon, today I would still be carrying a burden of guilt. The miracle of being healed has come with forgiveness. Had I not married an alcoholic and found Al-Anon, it is unlikely that I would have learned that freedom from the past is God's plan for me.

I LEARNED TO LOVE

I am the wife of an active alcoholic. In the time I have been coming to Al-Anon meetings, my attitude has so changed that it has actually changed my life. Of all that Al-Anon has done for me, two things are truly significant.

First, I have learned to stop paying for the consequences of my husband's drinking. Even before I began to attend meetings, I had sent for the pamphlet entitled *A Guide for the Family of the Alcoholic*. In it I read, "Love cannot exist without the dimension of justice." This impressed me, because I felt there was a great deal of injustice in my life. I went on to read that when a wife pays for the consequences of her husband's drinking, she removes the dimension of justice from her married life. This creates an atmosphere which soon can extinguish any love that *does* exist.

I learned that an alcoholic is a human being *in pain*, emotional pain. He uses alcohol as an anesthetic to escape from his pain. And it isn't until the pain he suffers *from* his drinking is worse than the pain he is trying to get away from *by* his drinking, that he will stop. When the wife pays for the consequences of his drinking, she removes some of the pain he might otherwise have to suffer. This deprives him of some of the incentive to take action and encourages him to go on drinking. When she assumes responsibility for his alcoholic behavior, she only increases his guilt feelings, which are already intolerable to him.

Paying for the consequences of a husband's drinking is no less damaging to the wife, because she feels she is being taken unfair advantage of, that her marriage is all one-sided. This leads to self-pity, resentment, bitterness and hatred.

As I looked at my life, I realized that this had been happening to me.

After our first baby was born, I joined a bridge club. My husband never took me out, and we never entertained because he was always either drunk or hung over. And we were always too broke. I felt the need to go out; I wanted adult companionship, and looked forward to my Thursday evenings playing bridge. But my husband would stay out and get drunk on those nights, and since I had no one to stay with the baby, I would have to call at the last minute and apologize. Then I sat and stewed until my husband came home, whereupon I would unleash all my anger and frustration on him

After I read the pamphlet and started coming to Al-Anon meetings, I realized how foolish I had been. A baby-sitter solved the problem very simply. I had always been afraid to get a baby-sitter before, either because we couldn't afford it or because I was ashamed to have her see my husband drunk. But since Al-Anon, I'm not afraid anymore and when my husband doesn't come home, I just call the sitter and go out and have my much-needed diversion. Since he has to pay her, it automatically removes my excuse for resentment and helps to relieve his guilt. And having to pay, even in this small way, adds to the unpleasantness of his drinking episode, and adds to the pain he suffers as a result of his drinking.

On occasions when I received gifts of money for birthday or Christmas, he would usually find an excuse to "borrow" it. There was always a reason—an urgent bill to pay or a necessity to buy. It occurred to me that if I hadn't *happened* to have the money, he would be forced to find a way to meet the obligations. For after all, the cost of his drinking far outweighed our bills. But his arguments were so convincing that I was always persuaded to hand over the money, and whatever I had set my heart on buying would become another frustrated dream.

Each time this happened I promised myself it would be the last, but it never was. My anxiety over the unpaid bills or the badly needed clothing would get to me, so that I would once again hand over the money—until Al-Anon. I learned that what I was doing only amounted to paying for the consequences in another way, and I kept myself from doing it, although it wasn't easy. Now he manages somehow to pay the bills and buy the necessities without my help, and I can look forward to a small luxury now and then.

These are but a few instances—all different versions of the same thing. But since Al-Anon, my change of attitude has already brought a noticeable improvement in our situation.

The other thing that Al-Anon has done to bring about this "miracle" of improvement is to help me see myself as I really was and am. I had been in Al-Anon several months when I began to take the Fourth Step ("Made a searching and fearless moral inventory of ourselves"). I never would have been able to attempt this but for the acceptance I'd received from the others in Al-Anon, and if I hadn't been present to listen to the stories that others told so frankly at our meetings.

I had always had a need to appear perfect before others and, indeed, even to myself. I dreaded criticism and feared losing the esteem of others if I admitted to even a minor fault. The last thing I wanted was an honest appraisal of myself. But once I began to understand a little of Al-Anon principles, I realized how foolish this was. These other members were admitting their shortcomings, yet they were still loved and accepted. Once I gathered the courage to face some introspection, I didn't like one thing that I saw! I had to face the fact that I was selfish, vain, arrogant, self-righteous, immature and wallowing in self-pity. In fact, I realized that I had been emotionally ill for a long time, even before I met my husband.

Through working with this Fourth Step, I was able to unearth a guilt that had been haunting me for years, and through the Fifth Step ("Admitted to God, to ourselves and another human being the exact nature of our wrongs") to get rid of it.

As I continued to study the Fourth Step, my self-examination revealed that my need for punishment had been the main reason for marrying my husband. This was the first time in our married life that I was able to admit I didn't love him, and never had. I had married him for purely neurotic and selfish reasons. Whenever a doubt about my love for him had crept into my mind, I quickly pushed it out with the thought that I couldn't possibly have put up with him all these years if I didn't love him. But now, in Al-Anon, the obstacles of pride and self-righteousness were slowly being removed. I faced the truth that it had been convenient for me to marry my husband, not only because it provided the punishment I subconsciously craved, but because beside him I looked so great—just what I needed to keep up my pretense of perfection. After all, people were so busy finding fault with him that nobody would criticize me, the patient martyr.

Then I found I no longer hated my husband, for Al-Anon had taught me he was not to blame for his drinking. I knew he couldn't control it although I still blamed him for not seeking help. But Al-Anon taught me that this is just another symptom of the same illness.

When I faced this fact, I suddenly felt helpless and ashamed. I had a great need for prayer, and turned to God, asking Him to help me learn to love. I thought, "How are my children going to grow up loving one another, loving their father—how can they even know what love is, if I don't know?" When I married my husband, it was for life. Yet I know that, having faced the truth, I could not live a lie. Prayer was my only hope, God was my only answer. He who loves us all, He who urged us to love one another as He loves us, surely He could help me learn to love.

God has answered my prayer. I am conscious of love welling up in me. After five years of marriage, I now love my husband despite the fact that he is still drinking and our life is still very difficult at times. I have begun to see many beautiful and admirable things in him. I care for him as a person, I feel a new warmth and compassion for him.

In my earlier meetings at Al-Anon, my friends there must have thought me very good at the "detachment" that is recommended in dealing with the alcoholic problem. I was, indeed, detached, not from his alcoholism but from *him*. I just didn't care what happened to him. Now I do care, very much, although I am trying to maintain detachment from the illness itself.

I am learning to replace despair, unhappiness and resentment with hope, happiness and serenity—because I am learning what it is to love. I am grateful to be alive, whatever happens. Before Al-Anon, life seemed something to be endured until we could go to our eternal reward for all the things we'd suffered. I know now that there are many things to be enjoyed in this lovely world, and I enjoy them, minute by minute and day by day, building strength and serenity for whatever may come. Since I have stopped feeling sorry for myself, I've become aware of other people. I enjoy the fruits of friendship and bask in the warmth that such friendship can bring. I've learned to give of myself and am no longer so fearful of people.

For these, and all the many other benefits I have had, I am grateful to Al-Anon.

MY DAUGHTER WAS AN ALCOHOLIC

I am the mother of an alcoholic. I am also the widow of an alcoholic. Living with an alcoholic husband was grim enough, but trying to save a doomed child was an even greater misery.

Florence was in her twenties when I faced the fact that she was an alcoholic. I went through all the emotions that accompany such a discovery: disbelief, fright, shame, determination to "do something about it" and despair. I tried persuasion, bribery, withholding favors, hospitalization, psychiatry and much prayer. Nothing worked. I talked to a member of AA, and he advised me to "throw my daughter out" and thus force her to hit bottom and face up to her problem. He warned me that she might die if I did this, but he also said she would certainly die if I did not. After much soul-searching, I told her she would have to leave home unless she was willing to accept some kind of help with her problem. I told her I would co-operate in any effort, but that we couldn't drift along as we were.

She left home and moved to another city, where she stayed with a friend and made half-hearted attempts to find work. (She was a qualified proofreader.) But after a while the friend telephoned me long distance to come and get her. "After all," she said, "this is not my problem. It is yours."

I went for her, determined to use this crisis to get her to seek help. She refused, but finally did agree to go into a a hospital for a "physical check-up." The hospital was a psychiatric institution and they tried to establish some sort of basis for treatment but she refused to talk and, after a few weeks, she left.

I didn't know where she was for a while. At that time a younger daughter was getting married, and we all wanted Florence at the wedding. I hoped this might be a means of getting her back into the family. It is all very well to advocate allowing an alcoholic to fend for himself and suffer the consequences of his illness, but when the alcoholic is a young girl, the feeling of responsibility transcends all else. I wanted terribly to have her home again.

We were able to locate her and she returned. She was in pitful condition, almost in rags, and I promised to take care of her until she could find a job. We set off on another round of trial and disappointment. She moved in with another friend, but her drinking continued until she had what the doctor later called a "post-alcoholic spasm." The young woman with whom she was sharing an apartment called me to come for my daughter. "This is not my problem," she said. "It is yours."

Again I went for Florence and brought her to my tiny apartment. Again I was able to get her to a doctor, who found her in frightening physical condition. I was able to get another small apartment in the building where I live and I fixed it up for her with furniture from our old home. I thought she might be happier in a home of her own, and she was near enough so that I could give her at least one good meal a day. When she got a job, I thought all would be well. But her drinking caused her to be dismissed and she was again drifting, watching TV all day and drinking. Finally, I "hit bottom." I didn't know what else I could do or where to turn.

As I lay on the bed weeping, I began to remember having

read an article about a group for families of alcoholics, and I decided to find them. I called the AA office, and after the girl at the other end of the line was convinced that I was not the alcoholic, she gave me a number to call.

The woman I called was understanding and helpful. She invited me to a meeting to be held the next day, and when she learned that my daughter was still drinking, she said, "That'll be all right. About half our members have alcoholics in AA but the rest have an active drinking problem to cope with. You'll have plenty of company."

I was so anxious to get to that meeting that I took a taxicab and arrived early. But there were already a few people there. They were expecting me. I was seated next to a woman whose son was an alcoholic. We understood each other right away.

I listened to a personal story of the speaker. I listened to the questions and answers. But I said not a word. I was afraid I would burst into tears if I did. But I felt that at last I had found "somewhere to turn." These people understood my misery, my self-condemnation, my frantic search for help. They advised me to learn about alcoholism, and I followed their advice by reading all the books and pamphlets I could lay my hands on. They advised me to attend open AA meetings, and one woman arranged to meet me at one.

I arrived ahead of time and again was mistaken for an alcoholic. The first arrival was the leader of the closed meeting (for alcoholics only) that was held before the open meeting anyone could attend. When he arrived and found me sitting on a bench outside the door, he greeted me warmly and invited me in. I told him I was not an alcoholic, but he merely smiled and, taking my elbow, firmly pushed me into the room. Immediately, people began to arrive, so I decided to be quiet and listen. I might learn something useful. The fact that I said nothing didn't bother them any more than it had bothered the Al-Anon group.

After the closed meeting I joined my Al-Anon friend and her husband for the open AA meeting. It was wonderful. One of the speakers was a young woman about Florence's age. Her story was as hair-raising as any Florence could have told, I felt sure, and I left on a cloud. I would tell Florence about this group. She would be as thrilled as I was and would join and would learn the program and be restored to normal living and her own, very attractive self. For she was both attractive and brilliant, having graduated from college, *cum laude,* exactly six days after her 21st birthday. She was also beautiful before alcohol took over. She had a delightful sense of humor, was kind and generous and had all the qualities necessary for a happy life—except for the alcoholism that incapacitated her most of the time.

But when I talked to her about the AA group she had nothing to say. I did get her to agree to go to a meeting but she was on the defensive and was restless throughout it. She went to a couple of meetings subsequently, always insisting that I go with her. Members tried to talk to her and be friends, but she barely answered them and dragged me away as soon as she could.

Still, I hoped the seed had been planted.

She grew more and more morose and drank more and more. Twice I found her passed out on the floor of her apartment. Once the doctor arrived before she regained consciousness. Not recognizing the symptoms, he thought she was having an epileptic seizure. Later the doctor changed his diagnosis, but he was an old-fashioned man who thought drinking could be cured by signing a pledge. Since he was the only doctor Florence would allow to treat her, and since he was, medically, very fine,

I stuck with him. But even he could not persuade Florence to
see an AA member. He did persuade her to go to a psychologist,
however. I had high hopes, but later this person turned her over
to someone else, who also failed to make any real contact.

All this time, at my Al-Anon meetings and AA meetings, I
kept hearing that an alcoholic had to hit bottom before he
would accept help. I heard, too, what the first AA man had told
me—that it was sometimes necessary to create a crisis in order
to bring the alcoholic to the point of seeking help.

So I decided to create a crisis.

If I had been poor I could have said, honestly, that I could no
longer afford to maintain my daughter. But she knew better.
Let me say here that, although many times young wives feel they
could manage the problem if they just had a little money,
money does not cure alcoholism. *I* used to think that if I had
not been able to support my daughter, she might have faced up
to her problem. As it was, I tried to create a crisis by telling her
that I felt I was wrong in trying to run her life.

"You are a big girl and have a right to make your own decisions and manage your own life." I told her. I shall never forget
watching her as she sat on the couch, twining and untwining
her fingers and staring at them.

"What shall I do?" she asked.

"You must figure that out for yourself," I answered, torn to
shreds inside but trying to sound calm and detached. ("Detached" was the word they kept stressing at the meetings.)

"Just know," I told her, "that I love you and am as close as
the telephone if you want me."

I left her then and went to my own apartment to weep and
ask God to take care of her.

I had alerted the switchboard operator in our building to

keep in touch with her and let me know how she was. I asked a cousin to telephone her often and let me know about her. I would not let myself spy on her, and it was two weeks later when the switchboard operator called me to say that Florence did not answer her telephone. I hurried to her apartment, my heart pounding. I thought that at last she would let me call a member of AA. I pictured her restored as I had seen so many others restored. As I let myself in the door I prayed for wisdom and the right words to say. At the sound of my key her little dachshund began to bark. It was dark and except for the dog's barking all was silent. Too silent. When I turned on the lights, I found her lying on the floor on her back with her hands above her head as she used to sleep when she was a little girl.

She didn't move when I spoke to her, and when I leaned down to take her hand, she was cold. She was dead.

For a long time I couldn't attend Al-Anon meetings. The members' stories and problems brought back the days when I, too, had those problems. But I also had hope then. Now there was nothing to hope for. I wanted to tell those women how lucky they were to have their alcoholics—and hope. But I could never get beyond the rush of tears.

Most of my family and friends outside of Al-Anon begged me to leave the group, but I found I wanted to stay. Those friends in Al-Anon were still dear to me, and I felt they understood even my grief although they couldn't share it. They have helped me to accept this thing I cannot change with a certain amount of serenity. They have helped me to have the courage to change what I can—myself. I believe that God wants me to do something about the alcoholic problem, since I have had so much of it. And so I continue to work within the kindly confines of Al-Anon. I am often called for Twelfth-Step work with other parents of alcoholics. There are other tasks, too, for me. I try to believe that when I finally did "Let Go and Let God," He took Florence home, away from her pain and loneliness.

Some day a cure may be found, but until then, AA for the alcoholic and Al-Anon for the equally suffering family are doing a wonderful service.

AL-ANON HELPED ME TO UNDERSTAND MY WIFE'S PROBLEM

What can a man do when his wife is drinking too much, too often? If you're like I was, you probably blame everything and everybody, the world in general and your wife in particular. You curse the ill fortune that led you into a marriage that has degenerated into a one-sided drinking bout. You live with the threat of ruin—financial, social and perhaps even mental. Then finally your only concern becomes one of survival..."How am I going to get out of this mess!"

I'd like to tell a bit about how I developed the above attitudes—how I finally came to a state of mind that daily entertained the possibility of deciding between suicide and murder. That may sound melodramatic, but those who live with an active alcoholic will know exactly how I felt.

While not all husbands (or wives) of alcoholics come to the same illogical conclusions that I did, you can safely believe that they think and do many things that are just as irrational.

Alcoholism did not sneak up on our marriage without advance warnings. Indeed, all the signs were there. What I lacked was the ability to read the signs that foreshadowed danger. We both drank, but I never cared whether we did or not. During our dating period, I was as happy without drinking as I was with it. My wife-to-be was not. Since I accepted drinking as the "modern" way of life, I wasn't too disturbed by her more or less constant desire to be doing things that involved drinking. In fact, I even admired her ability to keep up with the best of the two-fisted drinkers that we knew. The drinking I saw in her home was far in excess of anything I knew in my own, but this, too, I accepted as an aspect of the modern times in which we lived.

We met and married shortly after World War II, and I actually believed that she, along with the rest of the world, would require only a year or two to return to normal.

Our troubles with alcohol began within the first month of our marriage, and never stopped until she took her last drink. I could never understand why alcohol was such an important part of her life. It took priority on the shopping list, was included before, during and after as many meals as could be arranged. Our friends were selected for their liberal atitudes toward living it up. Somewhat stupidly, I could not see the pattern as a whole. I was annoyed when her social drinking got to the point that she sometimes "fell asleep" at parties, but was inclined to overlook its seriousness because I felt that everyone drank a little too much at one time or another. I really wouldn't mind her passing out occasionally (I thought) if she would only knock off the nonsensical drinking at home. These seemed to me two separate and distinct problems, to be considered and handled in different ways.

The years dragged on and our problems grew along with them. We argued more and more about her drinking. I had forbidden her free-drinking family to come to my house any way but sober. Finally, after five years of it all, we decided to call it quits. A three-month trial separation found us just as miserable apart as we were together, so a compromise was reached: she would stop drinking and I would allow her to come back home!

It required but a few short weeks to realize that success under this plan would be unlikely, but we were together again, and I just couldn't figure a way to get her to leave again. Separation would mean maintaining the home and supporting my wife elsewhere. That would have been tough enough on my limited salary. Divorce would have been a financial disaster. And this was only the practical side of the problem; the emotional one was an even bigger trouble. I decided to ride the storm a little longer.

As might have been expected, things got worse, but to a degree that I was quite unprepared for. By now the word "alcoholic" cropped up now and then, but we both dismissed it because to us it was associated with skid row. As bad as it was, she wasn't down that far—or so I thought. It would still be a while before we learned that one could hit the skids within the walls of a perfectly respectable home.

How bad did it get? From a daily drinker who sometimes drank too much, she had run downhill to a desperate, bottle-hiding neurotic who could go for weeks without ever really sobering up. Mornings were all the same near the end. She would sit on the edge of the bed, shaking so badly that she couldn't hold a cup of coffee, just waiting for me to leave for work so she could get to her bottle to calm the shakes.

When it seemed that it could get no worse, a miracle happened for us. At the end of one of her classic drinking bouts she looked at me and said: "I need help. I can't go on like this." Trite? Maybe it sounds so out of context, but in ten years of marriage it was the first time I had ever heard her admit that her drinking was a problem! She may have thought so herself, but she had never let me in on it.

An unseen hand that you may call whatever you please guided us along a winding path that day, and somehow we wound up that evening at a local AA meeting. Her biggest problem was about to come to an end. Mine was just beginning.

Many of the things I had blamed on her drinking, I was to discover, were of some other origin. In short, I was soon to learn that I had lost my whipping boy—that I could no longer rationalize my own shortcomings in terms of problems created by my wife's drinking.

The following week I went to an Al-Anon meeting. I didn't go because I thought I needed help. I went because I thought it was somehow connected with my wife's AA program, and I would have done just about anything if it guaranteed her sobriety.

What I heard at Al-Anon made a lot of sense—six months later, that is! I really didn't want to hear that I was sick, too, and that I ought to take a long hard look at what I had become during the period of my wife's drinking. Such a look could only be painful, and I'd had enough of that. After all, hadn't I spent ten preposterous years with an active alcoholic? I tried frantically to get that across to those Al-Anon people, but slowly, ever so slowly, it began to dawn on me that some of them had had it much tougher than I had. What's more, many of them were still living with active alcoholics.

Failing to get what I felt was the proper sympathy and commiseration, I decided to continue anyway, but still not for myself. I came primarily to find out as much about alcoholism as I could, so I could properly direct my wife's AA activities! I was so successful with this venture that she began drinking again within six months. My Al-Anon world collapsed and I had to start from scratch.

I was only slightly more willing to accept the fact that her alcoholism could best be handled by her, in her own way, but I decided to give it a try. Instead of "we told you so," my Al-Anon friends patiently helped me get to my feet. With their help I began to see that my efforts should be directed at straightening out my own thinking so that, *together,* my wife and I could build the marriage that had never really got started in ten years. We have made progress—three good years since both of us saw the light in our different ways.

I still fight the resentments that built up in the never-to-be-forgotten dark days. I'd be superhuman, I suppose, if it never occurred to me that the drinking years were costly in time and money. But instead of brooding over what might have been, I can now understand that, since her alcoholism is an illness, it wasn't reasonable to condemn her for being victimized by an insidious disease.

Earlier I said my wife's drinking had caused me to wonder if I would ever get out of the mess I was in. Today Al-Anon has helped me to put the problem into the proper perspective. I am constantly amazed at the twentieth-century miracle that made it possible for *her* to get out of the mess *she* was in.

I should like to add that I am more than grateful to the unseen hand that guided us to that first AA meeting and opened the door of Al-Anon to me and to so many others who thought they were alone with this terrible problem of living with an alcoholic and not knowing what to do about it.

I WAS ASHAMED OF MY BROTHER

My brother was sent to prison for a crime he committed while under the influence of alcohol. For a long time I felt degraded personally because of him. I hated to walk out of the apartment and went shopping at odd times so I wouldn't meet anyone I knew. Every other Saturday I took the ferry across the bay to visit my brother. I am the only family he has. I never told anyone where I was going, and I avoided anyone who tried to start up a conversation on the ferry or the bus.

When my brother was released he went to the one-room apartment I had found for him in another part of town. I paid the rent. I would meet him every morning and give him enough money for the day. I was afraid if he had too much cash he'd go off drinking again. He made attempts to find a job, but it's hard when you have a prison record.

One day my brother asked me if I'd ever heard of Al-Anon. I didn't know what he was talking about. He told me that he had attended several AA meetings in prison and that he'd been going to some since his release. I was appalled. I certainly didn't think my brother was an alcoholic! Going to prison was enough of a disgrace to our family name, but to accept the fact that he was alcoholic was too much for me to swallow. He said he'd bring me literature the next morning.

Well, to make a long story short, I read the literature, and I felt ashamed of myself. I suddenly saw the truth. I had been treating my poor brother like dirt, and in my way I was degrading him. I had become a recluse myself and when I looked in the mirror I saw a bitter old maid of 28. I realized these things slowly. It took almost as much time to undo the bad as it had for it to creep up on me. I attended Al-Anon meetings to give me the strength to do something about myself and our situation. I learned that I couldn't protect my brother, drunk or sober. He had to stand on his own feet. My doling out money was only holding him back.

Eventually he found a job. That was lucky for me, because I later married one of his co-workers.

When my brother plays with his two nephews, I sometimes find tears in my eyes. I think of what might have been without AA and Al-Anon. This story is short, but it took a long time to take place.

AL-ANON IS FOR MEN, TOO

If every man with a drinking wife could know what I have learned, years too late, a lot more men would be turning to Al-Anon.

Men seem to have the idea that Al-Anon Family Groups are only for wives who want to get together and sing the blues about their drinking husbands. I thought that, too, at one time. But I soon learned. I admit I took up Al-Anon as a last resort—and I didn't have much hope at that.

My wife and I had about as happy a courtship as you can imagine. Lots of friends, dances, card parties, golf, theater—and always lots of liquor. Even now, after all that's happened, I remember it as one of the best times of my life.

After our wedding things went on pretty much the same as before with our social life. My wife worked for a while and we used to meet downtown for dinner, have a few cocktails, and go to a show. Then we were excitedly awaiting our first baby and she stayed home, making the house pretty, learning new things to cook, sewing and being generally the perfect little homebody. Of course we had drinks before dinner, and sometimes after, too. To both of us it was as perfect as life could be.

I can't go over the ensuing years step by step. I don't even remember when I began to notice she was drinking more than we used to. Week-ends would get pretty hectic, and finally my own succession of hangovers brought me up short. I decided I was going to quit. In my innocence I just assumed that my wife would, too. How wrong I was! I talked it over with her, and she laughed and said that if I felt I couldn't take it, maybe I ought to quit. So I did—just like that.

She didn't, and although she kept to two or three drinks in an evening, I noticed she showed them more. I figured it was because I wasn't drinking that I was more aware of how her drinks were affecting her. Things went on this way for a good while, getting gradually worse.

One night I came home from work and she had passed out. I hunted everywhere for the liquor or the empty bottle. It never dawned on me that she'd be cagey enough to hide the evidence. I was learning a lot about how alcoholics can outmaneuver us!

The next morning I suggested that she ought not to drink during the day. She promised she wouldn't. After a few more incidents, I began to worry in earnest—all the usual fears and premonitions. What would happen if she turned on the gas stove and forgot to light it? I feared what would happen to our youngsters if she wasn't alert—little kids get into all kinds of things. We had talks, serious ones. This wasn't something I could talk about to anybody else. I figured a man ought to be able to handle his own problems, especially when they concern his wife, a wife he loves and who loves him. But if she *does* love me, I thought, why won't she stop drinking for me? Well, she wouldn't. I didn't know she couldn't. She wanted to; she made hundreds of promises, but couldn't keep them.

I did the household shopping, had her charge whatever clothes she needed, and tried in every other way to keep her from getting money for liquor. She had sold more than half our wedding silver before I found out how she was getting money to buy whiskey.

Gradually her good-humored acquiescence vanished. Every time I mentioned her drinking, she flew into a rage and said it was my fault. It got so I couldn't keep my mind on my work, just from sheer worry and exhaustion.

One day at lunch my boss asked me pointblank what was eating me. In a moment of desperation, I told him. I knew he was a member of AA, or I might not have had the courage. I figured he'd know something about alcoholism, although even then I couldn't believe my wife was an alcoholic.

He gave me the first inkling of the kind of problem I had. He told me my wife was sick, that she had no control over her alcoholic compulsion and that she wouldn't do anything about it until her desire for sobriety was stronger than her desire to drink. He warned me it might take a real crisis to make her want help. That night he took me to an AA meeting.

I was so inspired by it that I went home confident that I had the answer for my wife. But she had an answer, too. It was "No." She stormed at me in a furious temper and said that no man who loved his wife would want her to disgrace herself by wearing the label "alcoholic." I insisted that she come with me to one meeting at least, not as an alcoholic, but just to hear what it was all about. She went along, but only to please me. It meant nothing to her.

Things were so bad that I didn't dare leave her alone in the evenings, for fear she would hurt herself or our child. I went to noon AA meetings near my office. At one of them I learned about Al-Anon.

The first meeting I attended had eight women and one other man. I listened, I picked up literature to read and I talked with the Al-Anon man. After my experience at AA meetings, I was less embarrassed about discussing my problem, and from this first Al-Anon meeting I went home determined to try the ideas I'd heard talked about.

The first radical step I decided on was to have a housekeeper take care of our home and child. I did this over my wife's bitter protests and renewed promises. I assured her that I loved her as always, but that I would have to put someone else in charge, for my own peace of mind, as well as for her safety and our child's.

I think it was this step that finally made her realize she needed help. She has now been in AA for five happy years. I still attend Al-Anon meetings, always wishing we had more male members. And we would have, if more men only realized how much they could accomplish by using Al-Anon principles on what seems to be a hopeless problem. More men would come if they understood that Al-Anon is a fellowship not only for women, but for the whole family.

I HAD TO COME FIRST IN MY LIFE

I am the adult child of two alcoholic parents, and my life is dominated by that fact. Until recently, I was not conscious of the impact of the family disease of alcoholism, and my recovery began less than ten years ago.

The last active alcoholic in my life was a man with whom I shared an apartment. Despite the fact that we were not related, my feelings and reactions to his drinking were as if we had been. I took on the task of straightening out his life much in the fashion of a spouse or a parent. I tried pleading, sweet reason, control of the environment and even violence to the point of nearly killing him on one occasion. I believe it was an acting out in part of what I could not do as the child in my family of origin.

My friend's illness was brought into the open by his employer but, unfortunately, his positive responses to treatment and AA were very, very slow in coming. There followed many detoxifications and rehabilitations. At the end of his stay at one center, the director pulled me aside and suggested I go to Al-Anon—not for the alcoholic but for myself. Because people-pleasing is a facet of my personality, I started to go to Al-Anon and open AA meetings, saying outwardly that it was for myself but inwardly to keep my friend sober. Sadly, there were many relapses after that, and with each I saw a bit more of how the principles of Al-Anon could and did work for me.

After about two years, a major shift began within me. Again, while visiting my friend at still another rehabilitation center, the director suggested certain new courses of action which, because of the support I had been getting in Al-Anon, I was able to put into practice. I stopped my own drinking and, equally important, for the first time began to change my view of alcoholism. I had up to that time seen it as my friend's disease in contrast to my own health (and, by inference, my superiority). I now acknowledged it as a "family" illness.

The relapses continued. It took almost eighteen months after a strong suggestion by a counselor for me to be able to ask the alcoholic to leave—and mean it. Perhaps even more significantly, I was able to take action without tremendous feelings of guilt. I had begun to accept the idea that I had to come first in my own life.

Today, although there are no active alcoholics in my personal life, I am still involved in Al-Anon. I now understand that my illness is chronic, but through Al-Anon and outside help, I am learning to live a full life, one in which I like and care for the person I am. Put another way, I have begun to see that I do have more than one course of action open to me. My behavior is no longer as driven by outside circumstances as it once was, and I am beginning to lay the past to rest. More often than not, I now choose the healthy course of action rather than the unhealthy one with which I have been familiar for so long.

There is one last, but by no means least important, change in my life. Because I can now emotionally trust, possibly for the first time in my life, I have been able to fully commit myself to a relationship with another person and will soon be celebrating my fifth wedding anniversary.

AL-ANON IS FOR GAY PEOPLE, TOO

When I came into Al-Anon, I thought it was a club to get the alcoholic sober through some kind of magic. At that time I was willing to pay someone anything to get my lover sober. I would even have killed myself if that would have helped. That was then.

Let me tell you a little about myself and my family. Several relatives had already died of alcoholism by the time I was born. By the time I was three, my father was a rip-roaring drunk. Soon afterward, my mother started drinking heavily—and my brother drank with my mother and father. They were often violent together, breaking up the furniture when they drank and fought.

By the time I was ten, my brother had been hospitalized twice for injuries resulting from fights with my father. Later he got into trouble with the police and became a high school drop-out. After serious trouble with the law, he went into the Marine Corps and was killed in action. I was not greatly moved by this, for most of the time I just felt "out of it." Next, as a result of drinking, my parents were killed in an auto accident, and I moved in with my grandfather to finish high school. About this time, I began to discover gay bars.

When I saw my first bar, I could tell that someday I would find the man of my dreams in one of these places, and when I did, I would add the zest my lover needed to really live a rich and full life. I was going to college during the day, and at night I would go to the bars. It wasn't long before I met the man I was looking for, but he was drinking heavily even then. Our first year was like the fullfillment of all my wishes and hopes, yet alcoholism was already taking its toll. We began living together so that I could watch over him. When he started to drink daily, I thought something was wrong with me. So I tried to please him by doing things he liked—but all he liked to do was drink.

After two years with him, I started to have doubts that it was going to last. Now my every thought was with this man. I checked up on him constantly, even paying bartenders to tell me where he was. This only made him angry. Soon he started to miss dates. When he did show up, he was often drunk and very poor company. We never saw a complete ballet, opera or show. My lover was now becoming very unlovable. I started to pray. I think I knew my lover was an alcoholic, yet I was so afraid to say it—*he was my life.* One night, after he didn't show up and didn't call, I took the action that has helped me more than anything else in the world! I called a friend in AA and told him everything. After an hour of my screaming and tears, he said to me, "Go to Al-Anon."

Those words were like gold. I ran to my first meeting. I arrived late because I had to have a good cry before going, but the people there were all smiling when I walked in. I couldn't believe it! I thought I was in the wrong place. They said, "You can't make your lover stop drinking but you can change yourself."

I won't say that I believed them—you know I didn't! I thought there must be some kind of gimmick to this whole thing. I found out later what this gimmick was: me. I can't make anyone stop drinking. That was the hardest thing for me to understand, but after several months in the program, I started to believe it. I was also starting to learn about self-worth. Being gay and married to a drunk, I never knew you could love yourself. People at meetings offered me their telephone numbers, so I took them and phoned. I even started to go to more meetings. I was truly getting better.

Now I am trying to build a strong foundation for myself. I feel and look better. The program has made me grow into a more responsible, mature human being. Going to meetings has helped me a lot. I have found that the program works best for me when I can identify clearly. Other gay people in the program give me the courage to stick with it. Al-Anon is for everyone!

I MARRIED A RECOVERED ALCOHOLIC

When I married my husband some years ago, he had achieved 13 years of sobriety in Alcoholics Anonymous.

Twenty-seven years earlier, his first wife and he, and my first husband and I, were part of a group of young people who played tennis and golf and partied together. This was during Prohibition, and we had many drinking parties.

As generally happens with such a group, we all moved to different parts of town and settled down to raise families. We heard about our friends off and on, and especially about my friend's husband. He had gone on drinking, and had eventually lost his wife, his friends and several important jobs. Next, we heard he was dying of acute alcoholism. Time went by. Then we received word that a miracle had happened; he had joined something called Alcoholics Anonymous and was on the road to recovery.

When my two sons were 13 and 15 years old, my first husband died. I was very busy for the next six years supporting my sons and getting them through high school and ready for college.

My older son was in college and the younger a senior in high school when I renewed acquaintance with my present husband. He told me all about his past life and what had happened to him through his drinking. He said AA had given him back his life and he was now a sober, happy, recovering alcoholic.

I became interested in AA and attended meetings with him to find out how it worked. I met many wonderful people, and to me they were all God's miracles. After six months, we were married, and I decided that AA would be my way of life.

My husband told me that his sobriety came first, before anything else, even his love for me. This I accepted. I was grateful to God and to AA for saving his life, for I knew that without sobriety he would die. I settled down to be a perfect AA wife. I accepted the fact that alcoholism is a disease. I knew there must be something different about the alcoholic because, out of all those who had shared our drinking parties in the old days, only three turned out to be alcoholics. The rest of us just quit drinking so much.

I felt that with all his years of living this wonderful AA program, my husband should be a nearly perfect person, able to cope with any situation. I knew that God had been very good to me in giving me such a fine husband, and I was sure we would "live happily ever after." My sons were glad about the marriage, too, and wanted it to be a success. They were grateful that I had someone to love and care for me.

The younger boy lived with us for six months before leaving for college. I continued to work to help both my sons with their education. My husband was wonderful about it, and wanted to help as much as possible. He had never had children, and I only realized later how strange and bewildering this new life must have been for him.

If I had only gone to Al-Anon at the beginning of our marriage, I could have saved all of us much unhappiness and frustration. I thought, of course, that I was doing everything possible to keep everyone happy, but somehow it didn't seem to work out that way.

Before our marriage, my husband had lived alone for quite some time. He was used to peace and quiet, and having everything orderly. During the first two years of our marriage it seemed as though nothing I did was right. I did my best to please him, but somehow I only managed to irritate him. What hurt me worst was the way he spoke to me; it made me feel stupid, and naturally I resented it. I took responsibility for everything that went wrong and apologized for things my son did to upset him. I explained to my son what I thought I knew about certain aspects of alcoholism, but as I surely didn't understand it myself, it couldn't have helped the situation. I was always trying to be a peacemaker, without knowing how. I realize now, since Al-Anon, that I was trying to do God's work without knowing what He wanted me to do.

My young son was very understanding about the situation, although he couldn't see why my husband seemed to run hot and cold. One minute he would be wonderful, and then some little thing would upset him, so he would blast out at us. We were always afraid we would say or do things that would cause these emotional outbursts. I can now see he was as confused as we were and was trying hard to be tolerant and understanding of us.

At this time I was still "taking his inventory." I felt that if he were working his AA program, he would be more mature. I also had a constant fear that something I might say or do would send my husband back to drinking. This would have been a horrible responsibility to bear. I finally told my husband of this fear, and he assured me that he was the only one who could be responsible if he drank. He said he would go to any length to maintain his sobriety.

I found myself seeking help from AA friends, always asking questions in a roundabout way because I was too proud to admit that I wasn't able to manage this new life.

My husband spoke at many meetings, and I was so proud of him and his many years of sobriety. I felt he really had a wonderful message to give to the AA members. If they would only listen to his story, I thought, it would help them use this wonderful program. But I wondered why, with all his understanding of the program, we were still having so many problems. I never looked for the answer in myself!

When our younger boy went off to college, I thought this would help matters. We would be alone, the boys would be home only at holidays, and surely I could manage to keep peace in our home during these times. I wanted everyone to be happy, but I just couldn't recognize that I was trying to manage everyone's life. I forgot that my husband was only human, like everybody else, and that I must learn to let our Higher Power do the managing. I was always asking God for help, but I didn't listen for the answers.

I had been invited many times to go to Al-Anon, but felt I didn't need it because I had never lived with my husband while he was a practicing alcoholic. My husband agreed with me. We seemed to think that only active drinking caused problems! It never occurred to me that my confusion, and the way I hurt inside, could be helped by Al-Anon.

When I finally did go to a meeting with an Al-Anon friend, I went with a self-righteous attitude. I was so proud of my husband's years in AA, and I let everyone at the meeting know about it. I felt sorry about the heart-breaking stories I heard, but could not identify myself with them. Despite the troubles I was having, I was so full of ego that I even gave a little talk on things I had heard my husband say, honestly feeling I had helped them and that they were fortunate to have had me at their meeting. How smug and mixed up can one get!

Finally, after two years of deluding myself that I was working the AA program, I hit bottom. One Sunday my husband was in a bad mood. I kept quiet because I was apprehensive. Finally I got up courage to suggest that he call an AA friend to help bring him out of his depression or whatever it was that was making him act this way. Well, that was the straw that broke the camel's back! He turned on me and told me in no uncertain terms that I'd better find a program of my own and let him work his AA program by himself. The bottom fell out of my world. Hadn't I been a perfect little mouse to this man, hadn't I always tried to be careful what I said and did? I felt completely lost and helpless. I knew I must find an answer or I couldn't go on.

Two days later I went to my second Al-Anon meeting, this time with no smugness, no ego, no pride about my husband's years of sobriety. I went for myself, ready to listen and accept whatever would help me understand *my* problem rather than his. I found my answer. I learned to release my husband just as the mate of an active alcoholic has to learn to release hers. I learned that I am not responsible for anyone but myself. I found that the only inventory I could take was my own.

As I continued to go to Al-Anon, I found my hurt gradually lessening. I am finally willing to stand aside and let God's will be done. I have also freed myself from anxiety and a mistaken sense of responsibility. I am not so ready to judge my husband. If he is wrong, it is not my problem, but his. I have learned to walk away when something disturbs me, just by going into another room and asking God to take over. I have made some progress in my understanding of the Serenity Prayer, and I now try to wait for the answer. It isn't easy because we always have an urge to help those we love, but I have learned that I can best help my husband by releasing him to work out his problems by himself.

I know I must work the Twelve Steps—a day at a time. I concentrate on the Seventh: "Humbly asked Him to remove our shortcomings." Believe me, this is a full-time job. Since taking my own inventory, I have found many defects of character. Many times when I have succeeded in releasing my husband, I turn right around and take him back. Then I find myself in the old squirrel-cage again, so I have to work harder on *me*. I feel this is a lifetime program, but what better way of life could one ask for?

I know my husband is working his AA program and doing a fine job. Things have become much better. It has been our privilege to be asked to speak quite often at Al-Anon and AA open meetings, and this has opened a new life for me. At first I was very nervous; I asked for strength to tell my story candidly, what happened to me before and after coming into Al-Anon. This was not easy, for I didn't want to hurt my husband, but I knew how important it was to me. As it turned out, when my husband heard me tell my story, he had no resentment. You see, he really does work his AA program and has grown a great deal without any help from me. He was willing to try. I think this is the key: just to be willing.

Since hearing my side of the story, my husband has released me. This is a big step. I have learned to accept his suggestions (I no longer call it criticism!)—and do so graciously. We have found understanding and communication through Al-Anon and AA because the two programs go hand in hand. Each of us must work our own in whatever way makes us feel comfortable inside. The nonalcoholic goes to Al-Anon to learn about the disease of alcoholism and how to live with an alcoholic, whether he is sober in AA or not. As AA is becoming more widely known all over the world, many more young people are finding it. Many will marry non-alcoholics who may find themselves in a situation similar to mine. Maybe in a small way my story can help bring them to Al-Anon to find a happier way to live with a recovering alcoholic.

MY BROTHER IS AN ALCOHOLIC

"My brother is an alcoholic," I said to the young woman who sat next to me at my first Al-Anon meeting. She looked at me sympathetically and said, "I know it must be hard to see the boy you grew up with become an alcoholic, but my dear, you can take comfort from the fact that it's usually much worse when the alcoholic is a husband."

Is it? I thought bitterly, wondering whether any wife's situation could possibly be more frustrating than mine.

My brother is an alcoholic, and this is our story:

Once he had his degree as an architect, he joined a large and successful company where his exceptional talent and quiet, impressive personality led to advancement. He married, bought a lovely home and had three daughters. He drank socially, though never so much as to cause comment.

I made a success in business, too, and lived with my mother in a comfortable apartment. We had an interesting life and many friends.

Then lightning struck. My brother's wife became ill, and after a year, he was left alone with his three children.

He begged us to give up our apartment and come to live with him. My mother and I were hesitant. He was in his mid-thirties, and we both felt that it would be best for him to remarry rather than to establish a long-range family arrangement with a spinster sister and a semi-invalid mother. But he pleaded, so we weakened, gave up our place and made our home with him.

When we began to realize that he was drinking more and more, we made excuses for him—the shock of having lost his wife, the sorrow of having motherless children, the burdens of his exacting job. We were sure that time would improve the situation.

We never learned what was happening until it was too late. For several years, his firm had taken an unusually enlightened and generous view of his problem. He was a highly competent and valued employee, who had had a number of years of service with them. They had innumerable interviews with him (all this we only found out much later), even offering him a leave of absence if he would accept hospitalization under AA. They even made a contact for him with an AA sponsor. He was cordial and agreeable to all these overtures, but he managed to avoid taking any steps whatever to get help.

Finally, after many warnings, he lost his job. Even while he was still working, I was forced to carry most of the expenses of the household. My mother and I did what we could to protect the children from his drunken rages, but all three were seriously disturbed, despite our efforts to give them a sense of security through our love and comfort.

When things were at their worst, I found a friend—a perfect stranger to whom someone had given my name—who took me to Al-Anon. By one of those *not*-coincidences that reveal the hand of a kind Father, the first meeting I went to happened to include a discussion of the First Step. I realized that I had involved myself with his problem in a way that wasn't helping him and was causing my mother and me unnecessary anxiety. I knew which bars he drank in, and every night, partly to pacify my mother and partly because of my own fears, I went to get him, half carrying him home. I always prayed that he wouldn't insist on driving; I was so frightened of being in the car with him when he was in a drunken state.

I soon had further demonstrations of the wisdom of the First Step. Friends of my brother's asked AA members to call him and try to get him to meetings. He agreed, but he never went. There was nothing I could do, nothing my mother could do, nothing AA could do— until he was ready to admit his alcoholic sickness.

Remembering what I had learned, I kept reading and rereading the Steps, reminding myself that I was powerless over the whole matter. No more dragging him out of bars; no more riding in a car with him because I didn't want to hurt his feelings; no more lying for him to cover up his drinking.

For a time, a brief time, it looked as though our "hands-off" policy was making him realize he must stand on his own feet. I could see him make a heroic effort to go through an occasional day without a drink (he never drank at home), glued to the television set or trying to read a book. I could see he was suffering, and when I couldn't resist suggesting that he call AA, he'd simply say, "I don't need that. I'm not a drunk. I can handle it by myself." But of course he couldn't. Things grew steadily worse.

I learned courage in Al-Anon. I learned to evaluate the whole situation and to ask for guidance from the only One who had sound guidance to give. Finally I made a decision—the hardest one I ever made in my life.

I went to Family Court, told our story, and asked that my mother and I be allowed to take the children, for their own protection and emotional well-being, and live somewhere else.

I still have horrors when I remember how I visualized his coming home to an empty house. I wanted to run back and explain and comfort him. I knew well enough that he was suffering, but the thought of us, and especially the children, put steel into my spine. We lived at a quiet hotel in a town near enough so I could commute to my job. He didn't know where we were, but we kept in touch with the AA member who had tried so many times to help him, and learned that he had finally agreed to go to a meeting. One led to seven a week—and we had excellent reports from our good friend who was keeping in touch.

All this happened years ago. After several months, we met him, by arrangement, at an AA meeting. With this clearer vision he realized that what we had done was the only thing that could have brought him to the point of taking the first step toward recovery. Ultimately we were reunited, but only for a few happy months. He met a lovely young widow who is now mothering his daughters and a new son, and she, too, is an ardent believer in the helping power of Al-Anon for living with an alcoholic, even when he's finally found sobriety, as my brother has.

THE WIDOW OF AN ALCOHOLIC
STILL NEEDS AL-ANON

I am the widow of an alcoholic. I became a member of Al-Anon Family Groups to learn how to live with an alcoholic; now I am learning how to live without him.

I don't know where my story really begins. Was it the day my husband was born, or the day I was born? The day he took his first drink, or the night when we almost didn't meet? Could it have been during our four years of friendship and courtship, our wedding day?

I really don't know. But this I do know: looking back over our life together and my life now, I am convinced that events were not just coincidences, but part of a plan, with pieces falling into place. There are still pieces, not missing, but out of place. When and how they will be fitted in I can't say, but I do know that they will.

My husband didn't just happen to be a victim of alcoholism. Our period of unhappiness and trouble was short, compared to the years others have suffered.

Six years ago I realized that my husband was drinking compulsively. He carried it well, so it hadn't made any noticeable difference in our lives; my only concern was for his health.

When he wanted to make a major change in his business, and asked me to help him, I agreed. Surely, I thought, this change would relieve the pressures on him and do away with the need for his heavy drinking. For a short time it did, but soon I found myself working longer hours, taking more and more responsibility. He wanted me to learn all phases of the business. I wasn't too happy about this; I didn't feel I wanted to be in business, and yet at the same time I was proud that he considered me capable. As his drinking increased, I had no choice. I was becoming resentful—the more I did, the more he drank. I realize now that the drinking would have been the same regardless of the situation.

I tell this to help substantiate my feelings about the "pieces falling into place"; without this experience I wouldn't have been able to continue with the business today.

As I was compelled to shoulder responsibility for the business, my resentments increased. Why should I have to do so much? So he could drink more and more? I had my mother's illness to worry about—wasn't that enough? And didn't I have to maintain a home? Hadn't I had to give up my painting, my last link to sanity? This was all self-pity, of course—a destructive frame of mind. I needed help more than I realized.

I had heard of AA and seen some of its miracles. I had also heard of Al-Anon, but I didn't think we needed *that* kind of help. Being a great believer in prayer, I turned to God. I prayed that my words and actions would be the right ones to help my husband, for it was he who needed help, I thought, and not I.

The time came when I admitted to myself that my husband was an alcoholic, and I decided to attend one of the Al-Anon meetings and see what they had to offer. A series of events prevented my going, and before I finally got to Al-Anon, my husband attended his first AA meeting.

He came home full of enthusiasm, and at his request I attended a second meeting with him and continued to do so for several months. Was this not part of the plan, too? I am sure it was. It was better for me to become familiar with the AA program first. When I had to become his "eyes" and read to him, I learned the Serenity Prayer, the Twelve Steps and the slogans, and something about the disease of alcoholism. I could see that this program outlined a wonderful way of life—one that I needed too.

After several months I joined Al-Anon and found the same teachings. Here was comfort in learning that I wasn't responsible for my husband's problem. I learned that I was as powerless over alcohol as he. I learned to treat him as the sick person he really was.

How fortunate I was to have been prepared to face his last days. The Serenity Prayer helped me to face whatever the outcome might be, giving me the courage to pray "Thy will be done," and to mean it with all my heart. The program also supplied me with the strength and knowledge to comfort others—family members, personal friends and other close associates.

What I have learned in Al-Anon has helped me through a difficult year, and it will continue to help me as long as I use it, living one day at a time, and asking God to show me His will for me and to give me the courage to carry it out. It isn't hard to ask for help when we are discouraged. We must guard against becoming complacent; we must maintain our conscious contact with the God of our understanding, once it has been established.

I have been asked, "Why do you still go to these meetings? Why bother? It seems to me you would want to forget." I certainly don't want to forget. I'll always need the comfort and wisdom we get in Al-Anon. I want to be part of the fight against alcoholism that continues on so many fronts as the problem grows. How? I don't know; that is one of the pieces that remains to be fitted into place. But I do know that my alcoholic husband has left me a legacy far greater than material wealth; through him I found a way to live that will help me all the days of my life.

A MOTHER-IN-LAW'S STORY

I will tell this story briefly, omitting the many agonizing incidents that happened while I stood by, helpless to do anything about the situation.

When my daughter married ten years ago, I was very happy for her, although I had one reservation about her husband. I had the feeling that he drank too much, but rationalized my thoughts to myself by hoping that marriage would help him to change. I should have known better, especially since my own husband was for many years, and still is, a periodic drinker.

My daughter never cared for alcohol. Perhaps she was deterred by her feeling about her father's drinking. After a few months of marriage, I began to notice a change in Ann and Bill. Not only did Bill's drinking not taper off, but Ann had started to drink along with him. I stood helplessly by and watched my daughter go downhill. I bought the AA book and learned that the alcoholic will only stop when he or she wants to. A baby arrived a year later, but Ann kept on drinking. She told me later that she and her husband, over their quart of whiskey a night, often thought of getting rid of the baby because she was interfering with their drinking.

Finally my daughter became so ill she went to a doctor. After seeing her physical and emotional state, he referred her to a psychiatrist. On one of my daughter's visits, she saw my copy of the AA book. She read it. When she returned home, she saw the psychiatrist, who told her he could help her only if she were sober. At this point Ann started to go to AA meetings.

Bill went with Ann to the meetings, but only, as he said, "to give her moral support." After three months he had to admit that much of what he heard from the speakers at AA meetings was his story. In other words, he took the First Step, and admitted that he, too, was an alcoholic. So now both Ann and Bill are working the program together.

Through all this, I naturally felt tremendous resentment toward Bill for encouraging Ann to drink. Luckily I had enough sense to keep my mouth shut and not blame him openly. I realized that if someone wants to drink they will drink, and I couldn't stop my daughter. After Ann went to AA she told me about Al-Anon.

I went to many meetings and found them most helpful. In reading the AA book I had learned about the alcoholic, but in Al-Anon I learned about myself. It was really an eye opener for me because I had never realized I had been so greatly affected by the alcoholism in my family, my husband's and my daughter's. Soon I could see that I was too emotionally tied to my family, and now, with an interesting job and wonderful friends, I feel that I have a real life of my own.

My daughter and her husband speak together at AA meetings, and my daughter often speaks at high schools near where they live. They now have a second child and, to anyone meeting them today, they seem like a lovely, serenely happy young couple, without a problem in the world. Bill and I are good friends—with knowledge has come respect for one another.

A MOTHER OF A TEENAGED ALCOHOLIC

My introduction to Al-Anon coincided with my 21-year-old daughter entering an alcoholic rehabilitation center, where she remained for one year. From Gail's fifteenth birthday to her twenty-first were the most distraught, hair-raising years of our lives. I say "our" because her suffering from alcoholism indirectly took its toll on my physical and emotional well-being.

I was unaware of the existence of Al-Anon during those traumatic years. Neither the two doctors nor the psychiatrist from whom 16-year-old Gail sought help suggested Alcoholics Anonymous. After she tried to end her life at age 20, she was placed in a sanatorium for a month's rest cure, under the care of another psychiatrist. Seven months later, she had finally reached the AA-oriented rehabilitation center that was to change her life.

During those seven months, she had been treated medically by a psychiatrist with disastrous results. Although he knew my daughter was addicted to both pills and alcohol, he still believed in giving her tranquilizers. But my daughter did not take the medication prescribed. Because of this, I was in a continual state of anxiety. As a result, medication was put under my care. I took responsibility for regulating the doses. I wanted to believe in this treatment but I could not.

One day I came across an article in the *New York Times* telling of an 118-acre rehabilitation center, in a rural setting, which offered help to alcoholics or addicts. One glaring sentence caught my attention, "...the No. 1 rule is no drugs or alcohol." With this information, I spoke to Gail's psychiatrist. Perhaps it was a coincidence, perhaps not, but he said he had had this specific rehabilitation center in mind—but as a "last resort."

Soon, a moment of truth occurred. One evening my daughter sat quietly in her rocking chair and asked me, "Mom, am I really a sick person?" and I answered, "Yes, you are!" Not wanting her to feel alienated, I said, "I am, too, but in a different way." I told her we were shortly going to visit a certain place in the country where people can get help when they are sick.

She accepted that we were to visit the center, but getting her there was "touch and go" all the way. Over and over, she said she could not make it out the front door and down the steps as her legs would not support her. This was understandable because she was literally spent from a two-day binge during which, in her rage, she had repeatedly punctured her thighs with a sharp pair of scissors. A fear like ice gripped me. I felt death closing in, and my urgency in getting her to the center was also motivated by the memory of her past convulsions. Because I had had no sleep in 48 hours, I inwardly prayed for the strength to carry her down those stairs. Surprising strength came to me that day, and the feat was accomplished.

We both arrived in a state of exhaustion, and Gail was put to bed immediately. The Director asked me not to have any contact with her for three months. After that, we were permitted to write to one another. It was this correspondence that showed how far she had progressed through the program of Alcoholics Anonymous.

She experienced her last convulsion the night she entered the center. But this time, she remembered the pain from her convulsion. The assistance she received at the center differed from mine because they did not let Gail forget the experience. They walked her, gave her cold baths and kept her awake and aware. Months later, when she related that experience, she told me it was a major turning point in her life and that her desire never to relive that scene strongly motivated her to embrace the AA program. Then I saw the difference between my well-intended help and theirs.

The convulsions she had had at home were so thoroughly covered up by me that she could not remember them the next day. I massaged her, poured honey down her throat, soothed her and applied cold compresses. It proved futile to tell her what had occurred because, within a short time, the drinking began again. It is now clear to me that it is necessary for the alcoholic to feel the pain. But it was I who bore my daughter's pain. I deprived her of some of the incentive to take constructive action for the consequences of her drinking. In essence, I took on the responsibility and the consequences of her disease.

At the suggestion of a counselor at the rehabilitation center, I began to attend Al-Anon meetings. I was aware I was physically exhausted, but I had no idea of the extent of the emotional damage I had suffered from the family disease.

My parents and relatives were, of course, unaware of the "family disease" concept of Al-Anon and were puzzled that I, too, went to meetings. They felt I should be happy and relieved that my daughter now had a chance for rehabilitation. Yes, I was grateful that the crisis had happened—but happy? They failed to see my worst defect, which was projection, or planning the outcome. I thought, "What if this one-year treatment at the rural center doesn't work, then what?" and, "Where will I get more money to help my daughter, since every cent I have is going into her stay there?" I was financially and spiritually depleted.

This mess of circling thoughts was what I imagined to be constructive thinking. I felt that if I planned a possible negative outcome from the situation, then I would be stoically prepared for the worst! But I began to realize I'd been going to Al-Anon about six months and I was still obsessed with the alcoholic. Nothing mattered to me but HER recovery! As I took my own personal inventory with the Fourth Step, I saw that I had not grown. What was I doing wrong? From all the letters I had received from my daughter and my first visit with her in six months, I concluded that Gail had grown tremendously and I was standing still.

Gail seemed to have grasped the AA program, and when she wrote to tell me of her excitement in giving her first talk at an AA meeting before many members, I was so proud of her. Again I shared her happiness when she wrote that she had accepted responsibility for originating the rehabilitation center's first library. Clearly, Gail was now on her way, but where was my growth if my happiness was always measured through hers? I had no identity. I no longer really knew who I was. I could see I had not "found myself" but existed solely to live through HER life, HER feelings.

I badly wanted to work the program. As I reflected upon my daughter's growth and my lack of it, a sentence flashed into my mind. When Gail had first arrived at the center, someone had put an arm around her and said, "Just remember that the beautiful part of the AA program is that you don't have to do it all alone." I thought this meant the "togetherness" that alcoholics have with one another in AA. Now I realized it went much deeper! My daughter could rely on her Higher Power for strength and courage to live one day at a time.

Even though I had been going to many Al-Anon meetings, I had not "let go and let God" but had gone right home to resume my beloved *planning* and *worrying* routine. It was a revelation when I finally realized that I, too, was not alone. I was relieved of the burden of my own self-power! This was my turning point. Each time a circling thought of the future entered my mind, I repeated the Serenity Prayer to myself—ten times if necessary.

Although there were times I felt left out at Al-Anon meetings because I was the parent of an alcoholic teenager and the focus seemed centered upon the problems of the spouses of alcoholics, I soon realized that even though attitudes differed, the *effects* of the damage done to the non-alcoholic were the same.

Thus, it was the universal view of alcoholism that kept me going to meetings, regardless of personal identity. I noticed that my brimming eyes and nervous, twitching hands were the same as those of the distraught spouse. Here I saw the common denominator in the fellowship: the compassion that unites human beings caught in the trap of alcoholism. I could now see that my former attitude of uniqueness had worked against me. It had divided me from the fellowship rather than uniting me with it.

As soon as I could let go of my daughter—and what I had thought to be the uniqueness of her illness and mine—I could move on to the real focus of Al-Anon: myself. I learned to concentrate on my own maturation by focusing my attention inward to further my growth and recovery. Al-Anon was the mirror into which I painfully peered when I took the Fourth Step. I reminded myself that I must face and accept this pain before I could grow. I observed that all growth is accompanied by *resistance*, whether it is a seed struggling through compacted earth, the birth of a newborn, or a person's effort to surrender negative views. Al-Anon has shown me not to fear this inner upheaval, and I have personally defined it as "an inevitable process of growth."

Al-Anon helped me to think clearly. But it was a revelation to find that I also need not think at all, but simply allow things to happen. I had not realized the freedom of mind we all possess but are unaware of. If a problem was too complicated, I could "let go" and empty my mind of all thought. I found through Al-Anon that I have the choice to control my thoughts.

I have observed that new thoughts I absorb in Al-Anon are responsible for a change in my attitude. It then seems to follow that my behavior alters for the better. This, in turn, has a beneficial effect upon any situation.

Before Al-Anon, I would rush in to alter a situation and make no effort to change my behavior or attitude. I have since realized that I first have to change my thoughts and then the process will follow in a normal sequence.

Now I face the frustrations of everyday life with a letting-go attitude, secure in the awareness that my detachment allows problems literally to solve themselves. When my daughter came home after a year at the rehabilitation center, the detachment I had learned through Al-Anon benefited both of us. It was a beautiful experience that we shared. Gail went back to school, learned a skill and accepted responsibility for her own life. With the help of the Fourth Step, I received the courage to go back to school. And the most recent wonder: my daughter married, and

I'm now a grandmother who attends college.

Today, we are both very grateful—and still aware of the valuable saying that no one graduates from the programs of AA or Al-Anon.

AL-ANON: HELP FOR DUPLICATE RELATIONSHIPS

"If you have been put in your place long enough, you begin to act like the place." This describes how alcoholism hammered away at my self-esteem so that I lost a sense of who I was and where I was. It is not my purpose here to recount the many years of my life with an alcoholic wife. It is enough to say that, since I was totally unaware of what was happening to me, my own personality defects flowered into permanent fixtures.

Looking back, I realize now I didn't have the control over my alcoholic wife that I thought I had. In the meantime it was my own life that became unmanageable. Despite embarrassments and upsets, accidents and injuries, arguments and anger, I developed socially acceptable responses to these conditions. For instance, when my drinking wife telephoned other family members long distance at odd hours of the day or night and talked incoherently, I diverted their subsequent well-meaning inquiries about her health. When I arrived late to a dinner party alone, I would explain my wife's absence by inventing an urgent family crisis that needed her attention. When she intended to join me on a business trip and did not show up at the airport in time for our flight, I would simply book the next flight and call ahead to my destination to explain away the mishap.

Outwardly, I was smiling and happy. I kept myself in excellent physical shape so that I could always point to my own well-being as evidence of the normality of my life. Inwardly, I could not admit even to myself the reality of my situation. I covered up, excused, accepted and conned myself into thinking that I could take anything and handle any situation. As a direct result of my denial of my problems at home, I duplicated them in my professional life.

I chose a business partner who had many of the characteristics of my wife, although he himself did not have a drinking problem. He thought himself brilliant. He had charm of a sort and he was extremely ambitious, professionally. He believed in working from 7 a.m. to 7 p.m., six days a week, and he admitted that the objective of his labors was to gain an unlimited amount of power. I was not exempt from his hunger for power. For instance, he insisted on joint signatures on all checks. Later I realized this meant that he could hold up his signature on partnership funds to force me into agreement on some other issue. Any of our staff who took time off for family matters, recreation or vacations were considered by him to be disloyal. He continued to carry a sense of grievance toward them long after the incident of supposed disloyalty. Some colleagues thought that my partner and I were the hardest-working, most diligent people in our field. Others thought we were crazy.

After years of strain beyond belief, I had given up all vacation time, exercise, and what remained of my family life. I reached a point where my shoulders were locked in place and I could not lift my arms above my head—the result of sitting, for days on end, hunched behind my desk. Meanwhile, my partner's wife was stationed outside my door as if to monitor my telephone calls and my workload.

Life became a nightmare for me, both at home and at work. I felt trapped by the alcoholism I lived with at home and by a cunning, driven man at work. Only after joining Al-Anon did I realize I had created duplicate relationships. I had been attracted to similar situations, which were eroding my sense of self-worth. I responded to the difficulties in my working life in the same way that I responded to the alcoholism at home. After many years of giving in to these circumstances, burdened beyond belief, I became physically ill. It was during a lengthy convalescence that I was forced to look at my life and come to some decisions about its future course.

When I joined Al-Anon, the answers to my problems were not immediately apparent. I lacked *any* courage to change what I, and only I, could change. Finally, I found my answers in accepting a Higher Power. Without such a Power I could not have begun to unravel the mess I had made. With this Power I could take the necessary steps to let go of the alcoholic and her behavior and to extricate myself from a damaging business relationship.

My life has become serene to a degree I could never have anticipated. My family applauds these changes. I lead a physically active life, and I am engaged in a stimulating and rewarding new business. My thanks for this life improvement goes to my Higher Power and the Al-Anon program!

I CAN BE HAPPY IN ALATEEN, EVEN WHEN WISHES DON'T COME TRUE

When my mother explained to my brothers and me, six years ago, that she was an alcoholic and would be spending quite a bit of time away from us to get sober in AA, I was bewildered, angry and secretly embarrassed for her. I thought that surely when the other members of AA discovered she was taking drastic measures to help her cope with a few minor problems, they would throw her out. I was afraid to admit, or even think about the fact, that my mother had a disease which affected the whole family. A year and a half later, when my mother suggested that my brothers and I attend Alateen, I refused. I told her what I had taught myself to believe—that I was perfectly happy with my life as it was.

I found it *very* frightening to admit that my own methods of coping (which I had relied on for most of my life) were not as successful as I would have liked them to be. My parents had separated when I was six, and at that early age I had learned that the best way to manage the pain and confusion was to shut it out. I had to escape into something else—for me, it was books and school work.

I used to dread the long talks with either my mother or my father about their divorce. I squirmed my way through them. My mother's behavior and my father's drinking (only after I was in Alateen would I allow myself to admit that he was an alcoholic, too) added to my uneasiness. My unspoken rule was: "Don't think about it." I learned to avoid dealing with any of my emotions. When I got angry, I never knew why. This was also true when I cried. My denial and desire to escape the problems were so great that I don't think I ever consciously connected my mother's stumbling and slurred speech, or my father's irrational behavior, with the drinking.

Shuttling back and forth between two alcoholics in two different homes, and coping *my* way, led to my own unhealthy behavior. I became two different people. When I was at home with my mother (a fairly strict parent), I was a relatively decent kid. But when I visited my father, who indulged us, I would turn suddenly into a spoiled brat without ever realizing what I was doing. Maybe my father felt guilty about the divorce. Anyway, I would enjoy feeling very sorry for myself. I was shy, quiet and had few friends because I never actively sought them. I almost never brought anyone back to my home because I could not count on my mother not embarrassing me. For all my attempts to ignore my family's problems, I sensed there was something very wrong and I demanded that my own achievements would compensate. I was, and still can be, a perfectionist. I found I could not live up to my own expectations of myself.

By the time I was thirteen, my self-esteem (which would have been shaky anyway) was very low. As I saw it, none of my good qualities really counted for anything. Secretly, I couldn't help thinking that life would be fine if only I had the things I lacked—popularity, the right clothes, a normal family. Fortunately, my mother, who knows me better than I sometimes like to admit, didn't believe me when I told her I was perfectly happy. She used every trick she could think of to get me to Alateen. There I learned a way of living that I had never dreamed of. For the first time I had to look honestly at my own behavior and my relationships with the rest of the family. I had to make decisions about what was healthy behavior and what was not.

Gradually I accepted the fact that my "if only" wishes were not about to come true. But I also learned that I could be happy even if they didn't. And that was a miracle! In fact, the most important thing I learned that first year in Alateen was that my happiness depended on me, alone. I learned to be content, even pleased, with the person I am and a little more realistic about my expectations of myself.

Alateen taught me a whole new way of life. Now I understand the disease of alcoholism. I have learned techniques for dealing with the alcoholic, so that I can develop a relationship with the person behind the disease. I have done this with the love and support of my group and by the grace of my Higher Power. I know, at least a little, what it is like to receive "the serenity to accept the things I cannot change, courage to change the things I can and the wisdom to know the difference." And for that, I am very grateful.

LETTER FROM AN ALATEEN MEMBER

Dear R:

My father died at lunchtime today. When my mother got drunk last night and fell twice, Daddy and I had to put her to bed, and she's very heavy. Then at lunch today she went into a coma, so we had to half-drag and half-carry her to bed. I stayed to cover her up, and Dad went to the kitchen to sit down and catch his breath. I wasn't gone more than half a minute, but he died instantly of a heart attack. He's always had a bad heart and high blood pressure; coupled with his excessive drinking, all this was just too much. He had a smile on his face. He raised holy hell the whole weekend, but I was patient and good to him, and without Alateen I really couldn't have stood it. Every time he got especially mean I went and read the meditations, and that rebuilt my patience. He didn't bring home beer or anything else last night or at lunch today, so I was quite pleased. At least it all ended on a good beginning.

I was going to write you a story (for the paper), but now I won't get around to it. You can use this if you want. I don't care.

Love,

Susie

MY FATHER HAS A "NICE GUY" IMAGE: RELEARNING TO LOVE IN ALATEEN

My father has a "nice guy" image. He is friendly, generous, easy going and always ready to take his buddies out for a drink. He and I are quite close, in comparison to the relationships he shares with my mother and my sister. I always tried to please him and if he did not always acknowledge my efforts, I still knew somehow that he was aware of them and that he loved me.

As he began to drink more and more, spending more and more time with his buddies, he had less and less time for his family, especially his daughters. Things began going sour for us. My parents' relationship became unstable, and their marriage began to fall apart. My father would come home late most nights after he had been out drinking, and my mother would fight with him about money, drinking and driving, and his neglect of us. Sometimes he would make her cry; sometimes *he* cried. My admiration and respect for him slowly disintegrated. As our family life began to break up, my love for him disappeared.

I benefited from being the older of my dad's two daughters because I could remember the daddy of my young childhood more vividly, recalling this person with affection. Although I loved the man he had been, I learned to hate the man he had become. Maybe instinctively, I knew what Alateen has since taught me—that it was the drinking and the disease that caused the change. I lived in the past, tuned out the present and gave the future no thought at all.

Slowly I made the rest of my life as trouble-free as possible without really realizing what I was doing. In school, I did exactly what I was supposed to do—my grades were always among the highest in the class. I learned to avoid either trouble or too much attention. In this way I could be left alone. I didn't try to make friends, and those relationships that did develop relied heavily on the participation of the other person. Oddly and happily enough, I am still close to most of those friends, although it was not until I joined Alateen that I learned to give as much as I could to others.

My personal growth slowed down a great deal—I lost *years* as I let everything slip by, allowing things to happen without trying to change what I was capable of changing. I felt sorry for myself because I didn't have as many friends as I wanted, because my mom was crankier than other kids' mothers and because I thought I had no family.

It relieved me when my parents split up and my father moved out. Most times it meant that I now saw him without a drink in his hands. That made it easier for me to ignore a situation I had been trying to ignore for a long time. I could deny his drinking problem since I no longer lived with it. I could also ignore my own responses. When I was no longer exposed to evidence of my dad's alcoholism, it was easier to turn off my feelings about it.

I remember experiencing a martyr-like pride in myself for handling everything so well. I hadn't cried when my mother told me he was leaving for good, although everybody else did, including Dad himself—he was drunk at the time, of course! My grades in school remained as high as they had always been. I kept up with everything. Certainly I didn't notice any changes within myself, although I *did* notice changes in my sister. She began hanging out with an older crowd, repeatedly disobeying my mother. Even when she came home drunk, my mother did not seem to notice. So I thought to myself, "She's always been a little rebellious—so there's nothing wrong." I really believed I was handling it very well. The truth was, I was handling it the only way I knew how.

Coming into Alateen was, in a sense, an acknowledgment that everything wasn't as peachy as I would have had myself believe. I was in the program for quite a while before I really took the First Step by acknowledging that my life was unmanageable. I don't remember how long it took before I stopped resenting and hating my father and remembered that I loved him. And it was even longer before I began to feel as if knowing that I did love him made any difference at all. Yet I honestly believe now that it *has* made a difference. I am closer to my dad now, even with his drinking problem, than most of my friends are to their fathers.

I know that my relationship with my dad would have gotten progressively worse if I hadn't changed my attitude about myself and his alcoholism. Being in Alateen and participating in the program helped me look at my life and realize what I could and couldn't do about things that made me unhappy. I still haven't done everything I can—there's a lot more ground to be covered, but I know that Alateen has been leading me in the right direction.

SHARING CAN MAKE US FREE

I am a medical doctor, specifically an internist. I graduated from medical school with what might be considered typical training regarding alcoholism—twenty minutes in a psychiatry class. Although we were taught about the medical complications, alcoholism was presented as a manifestation of underlying psychiatric problems, not as a disease. From the beginning of my clinical experience, I saw patients dying of medical complications due to drinking. I had been taught nothing about the diagnosis or treatment of alcoholism. By following the example of my professors, I had learned to ignore it and to treat only the medical complications.

My personal experience with alcoholism seemed limited, but included an acquaintance with a popular professor of psychiatry who suddenly committed suicide, and a friendship with a fellow medical student who drank a lot of beer and took handfuls of pills. This student was hospitalized and eventually dropped out of school.

In my residency I learned to treat alcoholics as everyone around me did. They were the last admitted to the hospital from the emergency room—after all, the hospital was for "sick" people. I'd tell alcoholics they'd better cut back on their drinking. I was totally frustrated and discouraged because I had never seen a recovered alcoholic. The possibility that an alcoholic might stop drinking never entered my mind. I treated many patients for liver disease, seeing the condition improve while they were hospitalized and not drinking. But I knew that when such patients left the hospital and resumed drinking, they would soon return, even sicker. I treated one patient who was admitted forty-eight times for chronic pancreatitis. He eventually died. Half of my patients had drinking problems associated with their medical illness.

My post-doctoral fellowship required that I study one chronic disease in depth. Feeling the frustration of trying to help my patients, I chose alcoholism. I had no idea what I was getting myself into. I read as much as I could, and in due time proposed to my departmental chairman that I present a lecture on alcoholism. I invited a psychiatrist who I felt had written most intelligently on the subject. In the few minutes preceding the lecture, I heard the doctor say, "Oh, I have several members of my family who are alcoholics."

I will always remember those words, that moment. I froze. I felt panic. My heart beat fast, and I couldn't think. The whole scene is still fixed in my mind. I remember exactly where I was, everyone who was there and precisely where they were standing. I had never heard anyone say anything like that before. Somehow, I believed it was a physical impossibility for lips and tongue to utter those words!

It took me nearly a month to understand what had happened to me. This doctor had given words to something I had long repressed. I came to recognize that alcoholism existed in *my* family. This person's honesty had broken what I considered a taboo, a family secret.

Medical school had not given me enough information to diagnose my own family member. But perhaps denial was also at work. Even though this person had repeatedly been hospitalized for medical and psychiatric problems, no doctor had ever diagnosed alcoholism. Who was *I* to identify this illness as our family problem? I continued to study.

A few years later I heard a speaker, a recovering alcoholic himself, talk about children of alcoholics. I immediately identified with the problems he described, especially depression and difficulties in relationships with other people. I obtained a written copy of his talk. I was told, "Take it easy when you read this, Ken. There's a lot of dynamite material in here. My son had a great deal of difficulty when he read it." Because I considered myself mature and aware of my problems, I felt reading the talk would be a breeze. That evening, after everyone else was asleep, I began.

Adult children of alcoholics described their families' experiences. They identified common problems: neglect by one or both parents, parental fighting, physical abuse and/or incest. They mentioned family instability, separation, divorce and the unexpected death of a parent. I cried. In the safety of my solitude, memories of my childhood came flooding back. I remembered separation from both my parents, the feeling of abandonment when I was available for adoption.

Later, I began to feel highly motivated. Now I wanted to help do something about the problem. I attempted to speak with teenaged children of alcoholic patients, but the patient or the non-alcoholic spouse would prevent this if at all possible. There were many excuses: "The children don't know anything about the drinking problem," or "We want to protect them from further hurt." If I was able to speak with the children, they had difficulty confiding in me. I created groups for children of alcoholics, but no one came. In frustration, I called the speaker who had given me the copy of his talk on children of alcoholics. I asked him what to do. He said simply: "Ken, share your experience with other persons who have an alcoholic parent." For the past six years I have done this at every appropriate opportunity, and every time everyone has experienced great relief.

I once introduced myself as Ken, recovering "family hero," to a woman who identified herself as a "family hero," and we laughed. We recognized the roles we had played as children of alcoholics. We shared similarities. In Al-Anon meetings I find that same warm understanding. The open sharing at these meetings is something I have never experienced anywhere else.

My recovery has not been easy. It has been a slow process. But I have recognized and accepted the problem, and with God's help, I've become willing to change. Sharing can make us free.

FINDING A FATHER'S LOVE
THROUGH AL-ANON

If "home is where the heart is," then my heart grew up in a home with an alcoholic father. This experience, as the son of a problem drinker, has deeply affected my whole life. When I was young, I'd often wake up to my father's silhouette in the doorway of my bedroom, delivering a drunken monologue. Sometimes he would cry out in rage and I had to listen to a litany of curses. I remember those nights well, just as I remember the time I asked for love—his laughter still rings down the long, empty corridor of the years, echoing in my memory.

From my father I learned two tricks for survival. First, if your feelings are hurt, at no cost should you ever show it. Exposing yourself could only make matters worse. Don't acknowledge your feelings, even to yourself. My father numbed himself with alcohol: I did him one better—I numbed myself without it. Second, I anticipated every event and called it a potential disaster. This meant defusing and manipulating every encounter, all the time. Out of fear for the future, I charmed, I agreed, I delighted in order to satisfy, gratify, or entertain. If that didn't control events, I did an about-face and fled. It may have worked for the immediate situation but I definitely lost control over my own life. No relationship worked for me. I hurt those who cared most. I had done what I swore I would not do: I became the spittin' image of my father. Guilt, shame and grief gripped and held onto my heart. It was this never-ending pain that drove me to seek help.

One day, overcome by crying, I sought safety in a bathroom. There I helplessly prayed, "God, help me. I can't do it by myself." Amazingly enough, my prayer was answered.

Shortly afterward, I attended my first Al-Anon meeting. As an adult child of an alcoholic I felt as if I had found myself there, and I continued to find myself a little more each time I went. My depression turned out to be grief. I had cried over losing what I had never had: my father's love. I needed something to fill this empty ache that I couldn't name. Others at these Al-Anon meetings gave me a firm foundation based on the Twelve Steps of the program. Later I was to realize that God spoke to me through these other Al-Anon members. Slowly, my numb feelings came back to life. Thirty-two years of anger, pain, anxiety and fear poured out and, finally, from the depths of me came the desire for a relationship with my father.

Now, with the help of Al-Anon, I am learning to let God become my father and not expect my father to be God. I direct my questions to God—not my human, fallible father, whom I can now love. God has anwered my heart's simplest, most profound request with feeling, with faith and with an enduring "Yes!" I shall keep coming to Al-Anon to find the love for which I have searched so long.

ADULT CHILD OF AN ALCOHOLIC: GIVING MY WHOLE FAMILY A CHANCE AT RECOVERY

I was four years old when I noticed that people were not the same when they drank. My easy-going, good-natured father would turn into a mean, fist-swinging drunk every once in a while. I used to hide when it happened, so I learned isolation as a necessary part of my life at a very early age. If I could dodge the drunken rages, I was halfway safe. To me, the real problem was my mother, who reacted with anger and resentment for days and weeks after the drinking bout. There was no joy for her, so we were all miserable.

As I grew up, I remember questioning the erratic behavior and being given a quick back of the hand. So I learned what became survival for me: I started taking care of myself. We all grew up like islands, never touching. Christmas was an especially painful time, since it seemed such a simple holiday. If it hadn't been for the drinking, maybe the Christmas tree could have been trimmed without one of us children being punished, which always semed to happen. I became so disciplined at stuffing my feelings inside that I denied that I had any feelings at all. I was considered to be very tough.

Growing up like this distorted so many of my views on parents, violence, love and life in general. In order to escape, I left home at a very early age to be married. We had three children, and I promised myself that I would never raise them as I was raised. It was then quite terrifying to me to see the patterns of alcoholism repeated in my marriage. I soon realized that my husband had a drinking problem, and I took charge of my little family as best I could. After years of trying to control the problem, my husband joined AA. He, too, did not wish to impose the suffering on his children that he had experienced—for he was also the child of an alcoholic. It does not surprise me how perfectly we understood each other. Although only one of us was an alcoholic, we had both come from the same background.

I joined Al-Anon about three months after my husband joined AA. I was hoping to divorce and start a new life. But my first Al-Anon meeting made me aware that I had a lot to learn and that alcoholism was a disease little understood by most people. I came to realize that my own attitudes were sick and distorted, and I truly did not wish to pass them on to yet another generation. I made a promise to myself that I would commit myself to learning Al-Anon principles and philosophy and that I would not make a major decision for one year. I became willing to learn and, more importantly, willing to change. All of my children agreed to attend Alateen and Al-Anon in separate meetings in the area and give our family a chance at recovery by working through the problem.

Slowly, I have been able to turn my attitudes around. Only now, after two years of steadily attending meetings, can I honestly say that I have come to terms with the anger and fear that was so much a part of me. I have forgiven my parents for their behavior, knowing they were—and still are—sick. I can be grateful for the people in my life, past and present, who showed me the way with great compassion, even though my actions were so hateful and resentful. I know today they saved my life at a time when I wanted to die.

I am very sensitive to the sufferings of children in the families of alcoholics. I have dedicated myself to helping those families whenever possible, as I truly believe alcoholism is a family disease. The alcoholic attitudes have unwittingly been handed down from generation to generation by the drinkers and non-drinkers alike. *But it only takes one member of a family to get better, and life improves for the whole family.*

I am no longer guilty about the peace of mind I have earned. This has come about from using the tools of the Al-Anon program. I now realize that serenity is a gift to the family member as much as sobriety is a gift to the alcoholic. I love my family, all of them, very much. You see, when I changed and accepted the disease and its effects, our relationship changed to one of great warmth. I maintain my peace of mind by daily meetings and meditation on the principles of Al-Anon and by learning as much as I can about the disease of alcoholism. Life is not perfect, but there is much to be said for working through problems. I feel good today!

DISCOVERING A BETTER WAY OF LIFE: ADULT CHILD OF AN ALCOHOLIC

Looking back to the time when I came to Al-Anon, I see clearly that my life was racing toward destruction. I have learned through the Al-Anon meetings that this is the legacy of growing up in a family made ill by the disease of alcoholism. For me, alcoholism has proven to be a bittersweet legacy—bitter, because of the pain I suffered, and sweet, because if it weren't for that pain, I wouldn't have searched for and found a better way of living.

I believe that my self-destructive behavior before I found Al-Anon stemmed from my great lack of self-worth. From infancy, I had been emotionally abandoned by my parents. My father, the alcoholic in my life, was a very young man overwhelmed by life and its responsibilities. My mother was so emotionally battered from living with my father's alcoholism that she, too, was unable to express any warm feelings toward me. Thus, without parental love, I grew up far from well-adjusted. I was always searching for someone to love and for someone to love me, and without exception I sought out those people most like my parents. I was, in fact, perpetuating the pain of rejection by seeking love and acceptance from those least able to give it.

This pattern was to repeat itself countless times throughout my life. By the time I was a young adult, my self-esteem was totally shredded. I was hounded by feelings of guilt and inadequacy. I strove continually to be the "best little girl in the world." I lived in fear and dread that I would make a mistake or, even worse, fail. My perspective on relationships with men was totally distorted by my hatred of my father, which increased over the years with each incident of domestic violence or what I judged to be injustice.

When I left home, I believed that everything would be different. What I didn't realize was that I was taking myself and all my reactions to alcoholism with me when I left. If anything, life became more intolerable. I had merely traded one kind of chaotic living for another. When I had lived at home, I had blamed my father for my unhappiness. When I no longer had him to blame, I blamed myself. As a result of this self-punishment, I entered into a cycle of severe depression and self-hatred, followed by times of frenzied activity in over-compensation for my lethargic behavior.

It was during this period that my parents divorced and my mother blamed drinking for the marital break-up. This was confusing to me because I had never seen alcoholic beverages in my home while growing up and I didn't understand how my father could have become an alcoholic seemingly overnight. I eventually met a man who was recovering in Alcoholics Anonymous, and at his suggestion I began to attend Al-Anon meetings. At first I was reluctant to accept the help of the program. I wasn't convinced that what had happened to me while growing up had any connection with the difficulties I was experiencing as a young adult. But by attending meetings and learning about the disease of alcoholism, I found my answers. I learned that in the early stages of his disease my father had been a periodic drinker—that is, he drank alcoholically only occasionally and could go for weeks without drinking anything at all. My mother had protected us children from his drinking by forbidding the presence of alcohol in the home. Yet, although she had protected us from the immediate effects of alcohol itself, she couldn't protect us from the disease. I came to accept that it was my exposure to the disease that had so greatly affected me. I was now ready to focus on myself and my recovery from those effects.

One of the suggestions of the Al-Anon program is to get a sponsor—someone to talk to, who will provide guidance through the Twelve Steps of Recovery. I resisted that suggestion for a long time because opening up and sharing myself with someone else was not easy and I was not given to trust. But I did want to recover, so I prayed for courage and asked someone whom I knew and admired through the Al-Anon meetings to be my sponsor.

Our first meeting together was when I completed my Fourth and Fifth Steps—that is, I had prepared an inventory of myself, and I shared with my sponsor, as best I could, my feelings about my past behavior. That Fifth Step experience is permanently etched in my mind, for finally here was someone who was offering me total and unconditional love—that elusive something that had always seemed beyond my reach. Since that day, my sponsor has been a major influence in my life. She is the example I never had from my parents; she is the nurturer that the child in me craves.

ALCOHOLISM AND INCEST

When I was about three years old, my father entered my room one night in bare feet and an open bathrobe, and he abused me sexually. There was nothing gentle about this experience, for he seemed to be in a state of rage. I was left in shock and terribly afraid.

From that time onward I had many, many fears. I hated my father's feet. I even hated my own feet because they looked like my father's. I also had a great fear of any aggressiveness, especially from men. I changed from a chubby little girl with rosy cheeks to a pale, thin child with large, round eyes. I was frequently ill with many vague complaints such as cramps in my legs, stomach aches, and fevers, as well as all the childhood diseases it was possible to get. But I was always a good student and kept up with my class despite my frequent absences. I just couldn't manage to stay physically well, and I developed a reputation for being sickly.

There were enough sociable and kind adults in my life to convince me that a parent did not usually behave in this way. I tried to tell some professional people such as doctors or teachers who became involved with my bad health, that I thought something was wrong between my parents and myself. (There were other instances of physical abuse and inappropriate sexual behavior from both my mother and my father.)

Unfortunately, prevailing theory at the time had it that children fantasized sexual relationships with their parents, and whenever I tried to share my burden I was treated as a nasty little girl who made up stories. I argued to myself that, if these important people thought that about me, it must be true, and perhaps I was crazy. Then I did to my memories the only thing I could do at the time—I buried them so deeply that even I was no longer conscious they existed.

Years later, my father's drinking became alcoholic. Determined to make a life of my own, I left home and became a successful young professional on the outside, while remaining an insecure, lonely and anxious child on the inside. For some reason I did not understand, my friendships with men did not seem to work out. They started out well enough but they never developed into the marriage partnership that I hoped and longed for. Eventually I met and, unwittingly, married an alcoholic. I thought that I understood how to deal with his drinking and he was gentle, protective, and in the beginning, not very aggressive.

Suffice it to say that we became ill together, he by drinking and I by reliving a past that became more and more difficult to suppress. Again, I sought professional help only to be told that my reactions were inappropriate. They were inappropriate to the present, but not the past! Again, I believed these professional people, and again I thought I must be crazy. So, in order to keep my memories from haunting me, I began drinking, too. It seemed, in my mixed-up thinking, to be the healthier alternative.

Four years later and divorced, but still insecure, lonely and anxious, with little idea as to the nature of my problems, I stumbled into Al-Anon. I have stayed because the health and healing that have come into my life have been truly amazing. After some two years of trying to live the Steps of recovery, being a part of a friendly and caring group in which I participated actively, and having the love and emotional support of a fine sponsor, the memories of my early life came flooding back into my conscious mind in vivid color. The pain and rage were almost unbearable, but now, 40 years after these events, I was able and determined to do whatever was necessary to destroy their power over my life. I also sought outside help. My most important resource was my concept of a Higher Power who could heal me if I gave Him all the pieces. Also, I believed firmly that I was worth it. And I refused to believe anyone, professional or otherwise, who told me along the way that because of my childhood experiences I should be in any way abnormal.

Actually, my sexual relationships (including my marriage relationship) have more often than not been a source of enjoyment and deep meaning to me. Whether this was due to some healthy friendships with my peers as I was growing up, the age at which the abuse occurred, or mere chance, I do not know. But I am grateful that I have found through this closest of relationships the means to express affection, intimacy and passion.

My sharing with other members of Al-Anon has shown me that I am not alone in my experiences and, indeed, that incest is more often involved in the family disease of alcoholism than has previously been realized. But mine is a message of hope. Others like me *can* recover and live healthy, normal lives, enjoying emotionally and physically satisfying relationships. To achieve this goal, the love and acceptance found in Al-Anon are invaluable.

ALCOHOLISM, SEX AND COMMUNICATION

My story is not essentially different from that of any other man except in one respect—my wife and I were older than most at the time our confrontation with alcoholism began. (This was a second marriage for us both.) Shortly after the onset of alcoholism, my spouse became rather violent and abusive at social gatherings outside the home, and at the same time, we began to lose our ability to communicate with one another. While drinking, my wife became withdrawn, passive and quite uninterested in any normal relationship. From my side came anger, a sense of guilt, and inability to sleep at night, to work normally, or to have any kind of a touching, feeling relationship. This had more to do with my lack of desire than anything else.

I took out much of my frustration on my children. This produced an enormous amount of guilt within me. I felt that I was deserting them and they were doing the same to me, physically, emotionally and mentally. There was an unending succession of drunken brawls. This, together with the fear of losing our future as a family or any kind of normal life, took away any real desire for a close relationship with my wife.

There was no way I could say that I was managing, in any sense, to maintain a loving closeness with the beautiful woman I had married. She was two different people, and I was quite unable to cope. As I look back on it, it was the continual pressure of the love/hate syndrome that was at the root of our physical withdrawal from one another. I could not stop. I truly loved one moment and hated the next, and there seemed no way out. I am sure this resulted in the psychosomatic symptoms I developed. Some of them seemed carefully aimed at making it impossible for me to have a normal relationship with my spouse.

In sobriety, the guilt remained, and our sex life became stiff and even more unsatisfying. I was as demanding as she seemed indifferent. These sexual conflicts (among many other problems) resulted in a mutual withdrawal from the sexual relationship and, in two years, led to divorce.

As I look back, I see now that my failure to develop my own sexual identity has brought me much grief. Only recently have I discovered that my actual sexual needs are substantially below my level of desire, an insight gained from a lengthy period of abstinence. The sexual part of my life is one of great importance, but also an area of extreme vulnerability for me, particularly because of my fears of rejection.

For me, the key to a secure sexual identity is a strengthening of my self-worth through diligent practice of the Al-Anon program. As I work to fully assume the responsibility for myself, I believe the self-acceptance that I achieve will also promote healthy and fulfilling sexual attitudes in my life.

SEXUAL IDENTITY IN
THE ALCOHOLIC MARRIAGE

I believe many Al-Anon members have experienced sexual difficulties. Our sex life is a delicate and sensitive area, for it affects almost all we seek in a romantic and intimate relationship. Sex has been a difficult part of my life, not in a functional way but rather in attitudes and emotional responses.

I married at 23, and over half of our 14-year marriage was directly affected by my wife's drinking. Although the marriage finally ended in divorce, I am grateful that during our last two years together, my wife found sobriety through A.A. and I became a part of the Al-Anon fellowship.

I entered the marriage feeling a huge hunger for sex. I see now that this urge was activated largely by a very poor self-image. I transferred responsibility for my self-esteem to my wife and helped create a marital battlefield based largely on our sex life. Through sex, I was trying to win her approval and solve my self-doubts. I believed that, if she had sex with me, she must love me. After sex I felt great—masculine, strong and loved. If she chose not to have sex, I felt overwhelmingly rejected and unworthy. It is now clear to me that I was unbelievably immature and irresponsible in granting my wife such power over my self-worth.

Regrettably, I did not develop the ability to communicate effectively on these important matters. I acted as if acknowledging or even talking about these problems would make them worse. Consequently, as the drinking progressed, our sex life became, more and more, a silly but destructive game. To have sex or not to have sex became a game of rewards and punishments. I was in ever-increasing pain. I see now that this was the result of *my* abdication of *my* responsibility for *my* self-esteem and of *my* inability to form and support a healthy sexual identity.

As my wife's alcoholism advanced, these defects of character were disastrous for me. Most of the time, as I became pushier about having sex, her rejections became more pointed and aggressive. But her drinking caused confusing moments: sometimes we seemed to make contact and then reached sexual and emotional fulfillment while she was drinking. This led me to wish that she would drink—just a little, to help our sex life. I knew, of course, that she could not control her drinking, so I felt very guilty about these thoughts. While I hoped for truly intimate contact, more often than not there was a warm but passed-out body where I found physical release, but also great mental anguish for using her that way. During her sobriety, I was to learn that she remembered very little of these days.

In addition to or because of our own sexual difficulties, we both sought extra-marital sex partners. True to my low self-esteem, I assumed the guilt for both of us. I often think I became more obsessed with my wife's infidelities than with her drinking. Only recently have I come to realize that her behavior did not reflect on me. She was seeking relief from her own pain and made her choices based on her needs. For myself, my outside relationships led to enormous guilt. How could I resent so strongly my wife's behavior when I was doing the same? The lies required to sustain an extra-marital relationship also produced great discomfort.

Fortunately for both of us, my wife found sobriety in AA, and I found my recovery in Al-Anon. In our shared programs we discovered the true meaning of the word "confidant." Once again, we were able to share and love, and our sexual relationship was restored.

I can only urge others to recognize that, in the course of our illnesses, our relationships degenerate in many ways. But with the help of AA and Al-Anon they can blossom once more in an even more beautiful manner and take on deeper meaning for both husband and wife.

ALCOHOLISM, SEX AND HONESTY

When I was newly married, and long before I came into Al-Anon, I used sex as a weapon. If my husband was drunk the night before, there was no way I was going to respond to him the next night. He was a bad boy, and I was going to show him that his drinking was wrong and that he'd have to pay for getting drunk. I really believed that this was my responsibility. After all, if I didn't do this, he might think his drinking was okay. Once I joined Al-Anon, I realized how sick this thinking was. He was *not* a bad boy! He had a *disease,* and I was not responsible for pointing that out, condemning or condoning it.

I developed a problem with our sexual relationship as my husband's drinking progressed. For quite a while I stuffed my feelings. When I was pregnant with our fourth child, I could not enjoy our intimacies at all. I faked my response to my husband as long as I could. One night I was so disgusted with myself, I knew I had to do something. I remembered that Al-Anon taught me to keep the focus on myself. So I told my husband that I had a problem regarding sex and had not been enjoying our relationship for some time. I needed time to work this out, for I could no longer pretend that everything was fine. My husband did not like hearing this; he was angry and hurt. But I did not point an accusing finger at him or his disease, and I kept the focus on myself. So he accepted what I had said.

After the birth of our son, with my body and emotions approaching normal, my desire returned. I realized that, in taking a chance by reaching out to my husband, he could use the opportunity to reject me or seek revenge. I understood that and had no expectations. I initiated sex and found that I was not rejected. For a short period of time, my husband was blessed with sobriety. During this time, his desire for sexual relations lessened, and he was temporarily unable to perform the act of intercourse. After suffering quietly for a while, I shared my problem with someone in the Al-Anon program, who responded, "Oh! You too? That happened to us when my husband was first getting sober. It's quite common. It will pass." It did. I wish I had heard about this difficulty before we went through it.

My husband and I were childhood sweethearts, and for years I was never attracted to anyone else. But the pain and loneliness of his disease are sometimes almost unbearable, and at one point I found myself attracted to someone in the program. I reacted to this with terrible guilt, even though there was no affair, not even a spoken acknowledgment of my feelings. I was just fantasizing. When I finally had the humility to share this with someone in the program, I was assured that this, too, was understandable. It was an escape from the pain of the disease, and I wasn't horrible for experiencing this flight from reality.

There are times when I am not feeling at all romantic or "in the mood." I do tell my husband how I feel, realizing that he doesn't have to like what I've communicated. He has the right to feel angry or hurt: those are his feelings. Recently he told me he was angry with me. I thanked him for telling me how he felt. It was easier to deal with than silence or a cold shoulder. Al-Anon brings growth whether the alcoholic is still drinking or not.

ALCOHOLISM, SEX AND SOBRIETY

I am a passionate woman who is living with an alcoholic. I was brought up among very demonstrative people. This should point toward some of the problems I have had with my partner's sobriety.

We had some difficulty in our sexual relationship even before he entered AA, but now, after two years, the problems have escalated to total sexual abstinence. I have experienced complete frustration and despair—I have been desperate for a word of affection, for a hug, for a smile instead of icy stares and violent, abusive language. And this is sobriety!

I came to feel so unworthy, so repulsive (because I was repeatedly told I was) that I started contemplating suicide. All during last winter I could go to my Al-Anon meetings and cry, saying I wanted to die. I felt unloved and unwanted. What was the use of being alive? I found out that every time I felt like this and called on my Al-Anon friends for help, they reached out to me, showing me that they loved me and that they cared, that they wanted and appreciated me. My sponsor would tell me over and over again: "You are a beautiful child of the Universe. You have the right to be here."

There wasn't one night when I went to an Al-Anon meeting, feeling desperate, that I didn't come away feeling happy and alive again. The group would literally snap me out of my negative attitudes. First of all, I wasn't ugly. I had to learn to look at myself in the mirror and accept the *facts*. The facts were that Al-Anon is full of beautiful, stunning people, and many of us have problems with rejection!

It started to dawn on me that, since I was always attracted to withdrawn, undemonstrative people, maybe I was the one who looked for rejection. Possibly I was unable to face acceptance and sexual and emotional fulfillment. So I went for professional help. The alcoholic went for help, too, showing me that he *did* care. Repressed anger was responsible for most of my feelings of unworthiness. As I faced it, I let it out, recognizing its causes and only then being able to control it in a healthy way. You see, I was the type who never got openly angry with the alcoholic. I was a silent martyr, ready to kill myself without raising my voice. Imagine how a man must feel with such a saint in bed with him!

One night I really let the alcoholic know how I felt. While he was driving home, I screamed and shouted for all the nights I hadn't had the courage to do so. I even grabbed the back of his neck and shook him a little. He almost lost control of the car. The squeal of the brakes brought me back to my senses, and I saw with horror that for the first time in my life I had used physical violence. I was so crushed with shame that for a week I avoided my sponsor and my Al-Anon friends, until I decided to face it and speak openly about it at meetings.

The strange thing is that I started to feel better about myself because I was no longer pretending to be somebody I was not. It is true I had done something shameful, but now I was a real person, not the perfectionist nor the self-righteous martyr. The alcoholic did not appreciate the shaking but he did appreciate my being more of a real person. The love of the Al-Anon fellowship and the search for my true self had given me back my dignity. Since I felt I had changed, I expected—even demanded—that the alcoholic's problems be solved. I had a long way to grow because I still didn't see our problem from his perspective. I didn't see behind his fear of intimacy, nor did I know him. I thought he was doing it on purpose to make me unhappy.

Before long I discovered that another man was paying some attention to me, perhaps because of my new-found energy and self-confidence. I responded with an outburst of fantasies. I wasn't married, was I? The alcoholic had never wanted to commit himself, so why should I feel committed? This debate went on and on inside of me until I came to the end of my fantasies and saw that I was free to make a choice. Nobody else was keeping me from fulfilling my sexual needs with another person. But I could not hide from my feelings any more. You see, I loved the alcoholic and I didn't love the other person. I couldn't make this person love me the way I wanted, and I did not want a purely sexual affair.

Today I have decided to stay with the alcoholic, and every day I make that commitment. I have decided to accept him for what he is right now (he may change tomorrow or he may never change), to make the best of it and to respect him as he respects me. I will be happy, since happiness is "an inside job." I'll mind my own business. Since all I have is one day at a time, I'd better mind it well! Each morning I like to remind myself of that.

THE DIARY OF A COMMUTER

I'm a volunteer at the World Service Office, Al-Anon's headquarters in New York, spending as much time as I can spare from my job, which isn't too much.

Each of us, I suppose, has an individual view of the alcoholism problem that comes from living with an alcoholic. Somehow you always feel that your case is unique, until you hear that awful statistic—12 million alcoholics in the United States whose drinking affects the live of some 48 million others. Then you know you're just one of a big crowd.

Even so, it's hard to realize that the people you meet in your daily rounds may be suffering from the same thing. Nothing shows on the outside, so how can you tell? I decided on an experiment.

I commute each day from a small suburb to New York City, and I thought I'd start conversations with strangers I encountered on the way. It was surprisingly easy to bring up the subject of alcoholism, probably because so many of the people I spoke to were affected in one way or another by it.

These are a few:

Friday, February 1st. I was reading *Living with an Alcoholic* (recently retitled *Al-Anon Family Groups*) making sure that my neighbor, a tired-looking, gray-haired woman, would notice the title. I sensed her interest, put the book aside and smiled at her. "Excuse me," she said, "but I happened to notice the book you're reading. I live with one—if you call it living! He's in the hospital now, and I'm on my way to see him." I made an encouraging comment about so many of us having this problem, so she told me her story—a real shocker. I told her about Al-Anon and gave her a booklet.

Saturday, February 9th. Not a working day; I was going in to do some shopping. The noon train was filled with well-dressed women on their way to theater matinees, and one of them sat beside me. I noticed that a woman across the aisle had nodded to her and said a rather eager "Hello" to which she barely responded.

"That girl's been a friend of mine since schooldays," she explained. "After both of us married, we continued our friendship, visited back and forth—real close, all four of us. Our kids go to the same school, and they were friends, too. A few years ago she started drinking more and more until it was pretty unpleasant even being with her. One night at her house, she collapsed right in the middle of the floor. It was terrible! We left—and my husband forbade me and the children to have anything more to do with them. It hurts me, it really does. But what can you do? I told her a little about the disease concept of alcoholism and suggested that a little kindness and tolerance for her sick friend might possibly help her.

Wednesday, February 13th. When I left the station this morning and started down the street toward my office, I saw a middle-aged couple holding one another up, looking as though they'd been tossed out of a two-bit bar after a hard night. I still have a fear of drunks, and my first impulse was to turn and walk the other way. In that moment's hesitation, the woman noticed me and called, "Miss, Miss, please come here!" I had to grit my teeth, but I forced myself to step nearer to them. "Lousy luck" she said in a drunken mumble, "need a cup of coffee, help us, please." Thank God I'd learned a little compassion in Al-Anon, so I put aside my automatic thought that "coffee" probably meant a drink. Suppose it did? Or didn't? Their need was immediate and desperate, for whatever it was. I gave her some money and went on my way with her drunken blessings following me.

Tuesday, February 19th. A late meeting at the Al-Anon office; I took a 10:30 train home. As I started to read my paper, a man behind me tapped me on the shoulder, "Can I come and talk to you?" I turned and saw he was very much under the weather and again had that instant horror of getting involved with a drunk. "No," I said, "I want to read my paper." With typical drunken insistence he said, "But I have to talk to you." I turned around again, looked him in the eye and said, "I've just come from a meeting at Al-Anon, a group for families of alcoholics. *Now* do you still want to talk to me?" He said he did, and disregarding the amused interest of the other passengers, I went and sat beside him. It turned out he was actually worried that he was an alcoholic—his drinking was giving him trouble, both business and domestic—and he wanted me to tell him whether he was an alcoholic or not! I explained that only he could decide that, and suggested he go to a couple of AA meetings for which I wrote down locations and meeting nights. Did it help, I wonder?

Thursday, February 28th. Arrived at the office and went to see a department head on business. While I waited for him, I chatted with his secretary. I'd known her a long time but never anything about her personal life. And she had a story, which came out after I told her I was interested in Al-Anon. "My father died of too much drinking. I wish I'd known about Al-Anon years ago—I might have been able to help him." She told me he had been a good father, adored by his five children. "After he died," she said, "we all moved away from home. It may seem strange to you, but it wasn't my father we blamed, but my mother. She was always so proper and self-righteous, and such a martyr. As long as I can remember, she was always the one who started the rows that used to tear our home apart. I've often wished I'd known of some way to help him get over that suicidal drinking. I never even heard of AA until after he was gone. What a waste! And now I have a cousin—same story. . ." The next day I brought her some booklets to give to her cousin's wife.

Wednesday, March 6th. Beside me in the train sat a young man with a two-year-old and a couple of large suitcases. I tried to amuse the little one, and gradually the depressed-looking father and I began to talk. "This is about the end of the road for me," he said, "the end of what started out as a perfect marriage. We had everything going for us, I *thought,*" he said bitterly, "but just try to build a family life when the biggest thing in the house is the bottle. I'm taking the baby to my mother's." He'd heard of AA, and tried to force his wife to go to meetings; it didn't work. He'd never heard of Al-Anon until I told him something about it. Who knows what may come of it? Anyway, I tried to plant the idea that there's no such thing as a hopeless alcoholic and I hope he believed me.

Monday, March 11th. "Aren't you ashamed to let people think you're a lush?" asked the flip girl in bluejeans, sitting beside me in the train, pointing to my book, *Living with an Alcoholic.* I explained that the book is for people who *live* with lushes. She tittered, "Who needs it? I'd walk out!" "Not so easy," I said, "if you happen to love somebody who's drinking himself to death." *"Herself,"* she corrected me. "My old lady is really hooked good. It kills me sometimes, watching her fall apart day after day. It's easy in some ways, of course—she lets me do anything I want to, never interferes, and when she's had too much, I can ask her for money and she forgets what she gave me the day before. Still, I wonder how it would be to have her sober all the time. She was a swell cook, and she used to make all of my clothes. My father's left home. . . oh, well, I suppose that's life." I told her about Ala-teen.

Tuesday, March 12th. My seatmate on the 7:59 going in to New York was a well-dressed, dignified woman in her sixties—a rather unusual type for an early train full of businessmen and career girls. "No problem there," I thought to myself, but kept receptive to any conversational opening that might present itself. Oh, yes, she had a problem, all right. A son in the alcoholic ward of a state hospital, a daughter-in-law in psychiatric treatment for alcoholism, and she herself had the responsibility of her two grandchildren. "How do such things happen?" she wondered. "I feel personally disgraced by all this, as though it were somehow my fault." She seemed glad to be assured that no one is at fault, and I hope she found comfort in Al-Anon.

Monday, March 18th. The man I talked to on the train today told me he had just started on a new job at the age of 50, after being in business for himself for many years. It was a good business, but it had been systematically drained by a partner he had always trusted until everything collapsed in bankruptcy. "I knew he was a pretty big drinker," the man said, "but I never knew all the trouble he got into. I had to find out the hard way how irresponsible an alcoholic can be. It doesn't seem right that one man's drinking should wreck another man's life and his family's, but it sure happened to me."

Thursday, March 21st. I met a young man who, with the help of AA, had survived six years on the Bowery as a true skid row derelict. He was busily engaged in developing an education program on teen-age drinking for the high schools in his county. There wasn't much I could tell *him,* but we had a stimulating talk about the prevalence of heavy drinking among kids and what could be done to stem this rising tide.

Thursday, March 28th. This morning when the conductor bent down to punch my ticket, he remarked that he'd noticed the book I'd been reading on the train. "I wonder if you know anything about a kind of a group for young people with a drinking problem at home. We have some trouble in our family. . ." He didn't tell me what, but I told him about Alateen.

My experiment certainly convinced me that many more people need help than we generally realize, and comparatively few know where to find help. If, somehow, we can be open to people, and let them talk freely about it, perhaps many more would turn to Al-Anon. Let's not be ashamed to hold out hope to these troubled ones.

The Working Principles of Al-Anon

The basic ideas of Al-Anon, like those of Alcoholics Anonymous, are as old as recorded history. They are the concepts on which all spiritual philosophies are based. The same elements are found in the Bible as well as in the sacred literature of the Orient. These elements are:

Acknowledgment of our dependence on a Supreme Being.

Love for our fellow man and recognition of his dignity and value.

Awareness of the need to improve ourselves through self-appraisal and admitting to our faults.

Belief in the effective spiritual power of true personal humility and conscious gratitude.

Willingness to help others.

These ideas are the very substance of the Ten Commandments, the Sermon on the Mount and the Golden Rule. The working philosophy of Al-Anon is a pattern for right living, for overcoming difficulties and for helping us to achieve our aspirations.

We come into Al-Anon to solve the specific problem of alcoholism and its disastrous effect on our lives. We apply the basic spiritual ideas by means of what we call the Twelve Steps. These are reinforced by the Twelve Traditions, by the Serenity Prayer and by a group of concepts known simply as the Slogans.

It All Begins with Words

The mere words which make up the Steps, the Traditions, the Serenity Prayer and the Slogans may be read by anybody in a matter of minutes. It takes much more than a superficial reading, however, to produce understanding and results. The ideas contained in the words, applied to our daily lives, can bring about unimaginable changes for the better, but only to the degree that we absorb and use them.

They provide a key to spiritual enlightenment that has an almost miraculous effect on human affairs by changing our thinking and our attitudes in relation to others. They can, and do, release people from problems brought about by compulsive drinking. But we ourselves must do the work that brings these changes about.

THE NATURE OF THE FELLOWSHIP

Al-Anon Family Groups are uncommon people who meet to share a common problem: the effects of the disease of alcoholism on those who live, or have lived, with an alcoholic. In weekly meetings, members of the Al-Anon or Alateen fellowship share how they have used their program to recover from recurring symptoms of their own. Their willingness to discuss shared problems and solutions spans differences in sex, age, ethnic, social and religious backgrounds. From a variety of circumstances, they meet as equals. This self-help program of simple but universal principles led to their recovery and a satisfying way of life.

In Al-Anon there are no rules. Each member is free to accept or reject the suggestions of others. There are no fees for membership and attendance at meetings is voluntary. Anonymity is an Al-Anon tradition. Members are known only to each other.

The Al-Anon program is based on experience. For this reason members will often invite those who are, or have been, deeply affected by someone else's drinking to go with them to a meeting as the best explanation of how Al-Anon works.

Immediately, the newcomer will sense a warm and welcoming atmosphere among the membership which almost always leads to participation in an uplifting experience—at least for the time spent at the meeting. The ability to rise above the immediate concerns of life and to find a common experience is often how the newcomer first recognizes the presence of a Higher Power—the name given to the source of this spiritual change.

In A.A. pioneering days, close relatives of recovering alcoholics realized that to solve their personal problems they needed to apply the same principles that helped alcoholics in their recovery. When wives of early A.A. members visited groups all over the country, they told of the personal help they had received by living A.A.'s Twelve Steps of Recovery. This helped to improve family relationships that often remained difficult after the alcoholic had become sober.

Husbands and wives and other relatives of A.A. members began to hold meetings to discuss *their* common problems. By 1948, members of Family Groups had applied to the A.A. General Service Office for listing. Many troubled relatives of alcoholics were asking *them* for help. But A.A. was designed to help alcoholics, and not other family members. In 1951, several A.A. wives formed a Clearing House Committee to get in touch with these inquirers and to coordinate and serve the then-existing fifty family groups. As a result of polling each group, the name Al-Anon Family Groups was chosen. The name is a contraction of the first few letters in the words Alcoholics Anonymous. The Twelve Steps of A.A., almost unchanged, and later the Twelve Traditions were both adopted as guiding principles.

Alateen became a part of Al-Anon when the teenaged children in the families of alcoholics realized that their lives, too, had been deeply affected by someone else's drinking. In 1957 Alateen grew out of their needs. A seventeen-year-old boy, whose father was in A.A. and whose mother was in Al-Anon, had been quite successful in trying to solve his problems by applying the A.A. Steps and slogans. With his parents' encouragement, he asked five other teenagers with alcoholic parents to join him in forming a fellowship to help teenagers with alcoholism in the family. The idea caught on and the number of groups began to grow.

The logos of the Al-Anon fellowship each consist of a circle within a triangle. The circle refers to the Higher Power, which may be characterized according to the preference of each individual member. The corners of the triangle stand for the three legacies of the Al-Anon program. They are RECOVERY through the Twelve Steps, UNITY through the Twelve Traditions and SERVICE through the Twelve Concepts of Al-Anon.

The first legacy, RECOVERY, guides the way to a normal, useful way of life. The second legacy, UNITY, provides a framework within which Al-Anon/Alateen groups can carry on their affairs in harmony. (Both the Twelve Steps and Twelve Traditions are described in greater detail elsewhere in this section.) The third legacy, SERVICE, requires carrying the message—informally to the relative or friend of an alcoholic (known as Twelve-Step work) and formally through the structure of the Al-Anon/Alateen fellowship as a whole.

Although Al-Anon had its roots in A.A., by 1968 the Al-Anon World Service Conference unanimously approved the development of Al-Anon's separate Concepts of Service, based on the Al-Anon experience. During 1969, Lois W. chaired a committee that produced a proposed text. These Concepts were well considered before the World Service Conference of 1970 affirmed them as guidelines for service.

These Al-Anon/Alateen services maintain communications and take care of routine operations. They have only enough structure to assure effective functioning and free exchange of information and help. The Al-Anon/Alateen Group is the basic unit. Each group is led by a rotating slate of officers and operates autonomously, except in matters which may affect other groups.

Each Group elects a Group Representative (GR) to attend the District meeting and Area Assemblies. The District is a geographical division containing a number of groups located closely enough for convenience. Groups, represented by their GR'S, share information, and each GR can bring back to the home group the broader experience learned through the District meetings.

A District Representative (DR) is elected from the GR's who make up the District meeting. All the Districts in a state or Canadian province make up an Area (except in large or populous states, where there may be two).

The Assembly, composed of all GR's and elected DR's in the Area, meets at least once every three years. Each Assembly is represented by one Delegate at the World Service Conference.

The Delegate is an Al-Anon/Alateen member elected from among the DR's by the GR's who are present at the Assembly held for the purpose. The Delegate represents all the groups in his or her Area.

Delegates from all the Areas in the U.S. and Canada meet once a year for several days of intensive sessions called the World Service Conference. Discussions on matters of policy provide guidance for the World Service Office and Al-Anon/Alateen as a whole. Information is relayed back to the home groups through the Delegates, the DR's and GR's. The World Service Office (WSO) acts as a service center for over 26,000 groups all over the world. General Service Offices are the equivalent of the World Service Office in other countries. Several have Conferences of their own.

Al-Anon/Alateen Information Services (Intergroups) are local service centers established by one or more Districts to provide a listing of local Al-Anon/Alateen meetings, maintain and distribute Conference-Approved Literature and serve as an avenue for local Public Information and Institutions work.

Through this service structure, Al-Anon/Alateen offers support to its membership and unified information to all professionals concerned with alcoholism. Al-Anon maintains a separate but friendly relationship with the professional community.

The Al-Anon/Alateen fellowship has enjoyed accelerated growth around the world in countries where many different languages are spoken. Although it grew out of a need expressed by wives of A.A. members, this "extended family" now offers help to any relative or close associate of an alcoholic who feels his or her life has been deeply affected by the drinking. At least half the members of Al-Anon are friends or relatives of alcoholics who have not yet joined A.A.

THE TWELVE STEPS AND
TWELVE TRADITIONS

Al-Anon is not a structured organization. Groups and the decisions of individual members are entirely autonomous, except in matters affecting another group or Al-Anon as a whole. Al-Anon is held together by a unity of purpose. The ideas that provide guidance for individual growth are contained in the Twelve Steps of Recovery. Ideas for the harmonious functioning of the Al-Anon group are contained in the Twelve Traditions.

The Twelve Steps

1. We admitted we were powerless over alcohol—that our lives had become unmanageable.
2. Came to believe that a Power greater than ourselves could restore us to sanity.
3. Made a decision to turn our will and our lives over to the care of God *as we understood Him.*
4. Made a searching and fearless moral inventory of ourselves.
5. Admitted to God, to ourselves, and to another human being the exact nature of our wrongs.
6. Were entirely ready to have God remove all these defects of character.

7. Humbly asked Him to remove our shortcomings.
8. Made a list of all persons we had harmed, and became willing to make amends to them all.
9. Made direct amends to such people wherever possible, except when to do so would injure them or others.
10. Continued to take personal inventory and when we were wrong promply admitted it.
11. Sought through prayer and meditation to improve our conscious contact with God *as we understood Him,* praying only for knowledge of His will for us and the power to carry that out.
12. Having had a spiritual awakening as the result of these steps, we tried to carry this message to others, and to practice these principles in all our affairs.

These Steps have been adapted by Al-Anon and Alateen from those of Alcoholics Anonymous, with a few minor changes. At first reading, it may seem odd that they are written in the past tense. The early members of A.A. practiced these principles *without a word being written down.* They met to share their common experience with one another and to reach for personal and spiritual growth. The miracle was that together they achieved sobriety, healthy attitudes and peace of mind. In order to bring this message to other still-suffering alcoholics, the Steps were brought into focus and recorded. The Twelve Steps recount something that *happened,* how it was accomplished and how others using the same ideas can conquer their shortcomings and come to terms with life.

The simplicity of this program of recovery made an immediate appeal to family members surrounding the alcoholic. The first A.A. wives asked themselves if this same program of recovery that had wrought such marvellous changes in their husbands' lives could work for them. They, too, had found themselves powerless to control the effects of alcohol. Life had certainly become unmanageable for them. With the foundation of Al-Anon in the early 1950's, the Twelve Steps of Recovery were enthusiastically adopted. Now they are a familiar program for living throughout the world.

At some point, the newcomer grows past the immediate problems that brought them to the Al-Anon program. Instead of resting upon this achievement, Al-Anon suggests a renewed effort toward personal and spiritual growth. The next key is to increase self-knowledge. In the words of the Steps, it is suggested that the members make "a searching and fearless moral inventory" of themselves. At first sight this seems a tall order! But most Al-Anon members come to realize that they themselves have been forgotten in the midst of alcoholic turmoil and confusion. They rediscover that they are persons in their own right, with their own needs for happiness and peace of mind. Members draw courage from one another in taking this step. Invariably, they find not only the "defects of character" that they first imagined, but assets as well. Al-Anon members are all good people with many fine qualities only waiting to be acknowledged.

With this new-found appreciation of themselves, individuals are encouraged to renew their contact with others in a more effective way. The Steps suggest they become "willing to make amends" and put the past behind them. Once done, the way is clear to live comfortably in the present. Three maintenance steps are added: to continue "to take personal inventory"; to improve the conscious contact with the individual's source of spiritual strength, the God *"as we understood Him";* and to carry the message of hope to others who might be in need of help.

The Twelve Steps form the heart of the Al-Anon Program. Often a Step will be chosen as the topic of an Al-Anon meeting. On such an occasion, the meeting leader will share his or her ideas, insights and views, often illuminated with personal anecdotes regarding the family disease of alcoholism. Sometimes serious, sometimes light-hearted, all the members present are invited to share in the pooling of ideas with their own comments, from which all can benefit. In closing, members are advised to "take what you like and leave the rest." Meetings are broad enough in scope to allow every member, of whatever background, to come away with at least one practical example to use in the alcoholic situation, or one idea to improve daily living.

The Twelve Traditions of Al-Anon

As the Twelve Steps provide guidance for the individual member, so the Twelve Traditions provide a structure for smooth group functioning. They, too, have been adapted from Alcoholics Anonymous.

1. Our common welfare should come first; personal progress for the greatest number depends upon unity.
2. For our group purpose there is but one authority—a loving God as He may express Himself in our group conscience. Our leaders are but trusted servants—they do not govern.
3. The relatives of alcoholics, when gathered together for mutual aid, may call themselves an Al-Anon Family Group, provided that, as a group, they have no other affiliation. The only requirement for membership is that there be a problem of alcoholism in a relative or friend.

4. Each group should be autonomous, except in matters affecting another group or Al-Anon or AA as a whole.
5. Each Al-Anon Family Group has but one purpose: to help families of alcoholics. We do this by practicing the Twelve Steps of AA *ourselves*, by encouraging and understanding our alcoholic relatives, and by welcoming and giving comfort to families of alcoholics.
6. Our Al-Anon Family Groups ought never endorse, finance or lend our name to any outside enterprise, lest problems of money, property and prestige divert us from our primary spiritual aim. Although a separate entity, we should always cooperate with Alcoholics Anonymous.
7. Every group ought to be fully self-supporting, declining outside contributions.
8. Al-Anon Twelfth-Step work should remain forever nonprofessional, but our service centers may employ special workers.
9. Our groups, as such, ought never be organized; but we may create service boards or committees directly responsible to those they serve.
10. The Al-Anon Family Groups have no opinion on outside issues; hence our name ought never be drawn into public controversy.
11. Our public relations policy is based on attraction rather than promotion; we need always maintain personal anonymity at the level of press, radio, TV and films. We need guard with special care the anonymity of all AA members.
12. Anonymity is the spiritual foundation of all our Traditions, ever reminding us to place principles over personalities.

The Twelve Traditions of Alateen

Alateen chose to adapt the Traditions in a slightly amended form:

1. Our common welfare should come first; personal progress for the greatest number depends upon unity.
2. For our group purpose there is but one authority—a loving God as He may express Himself in our group conscience. Our leaders are but trusted servants; they do not govern.
3. The only requirement for membership is that there be a problem of alcoholism in a relative or friend. The teenage relatives of alcoholics when gathered together for mutual aid, may call themselves an Alateen Group provided that, as a group, they have no other affiliation.
4. Each group should be autonomous, except in matters affecting other Alateen and Al-Anon Family Groups or AA as a whole.
5. Each Alateen Group has but one purpose: to help other teenagers of alcoholics. We do this by practicing the Twelve Steps of AA ourselves and by encouraging and understanding the members of our immediate families.
6. Alateens, being part of Al-Anon Family Groups, ought never to endorse, finance or lend our name to any outside enterprise, lest problems of money, property and prestige divert us from our primary spiritual aim. Although a separate entity, we should always cooperate with Alcoholics Anonymous.
7. Every group ought to be fully self-supporting, declining outside contributions.

8. Alateen Twelfth-Step work should remain forever non-professional, but our service centers may employ special workers.
9. Our groups, as such, ought never be organized; but we may create service boards or committees directly responsible to those they serve.
10. The Alateen Groups have no opinion on outside issues; hence our name ought never be drawn into public controversy.
11. Our public relations policy is based on attraction rather than promotion; we need always maintain personal anonymity at the level of press, radio, TV and films. We need guard with special care the anonymity of all AA members.
12. Anonymity is the spiritual foundation of all our Traditions, ever reminding us to place principles above personalities.

Experience has shown that the strength and growth of any Al-Anon/Alateen group depends upon adherence to these principles.

Of first importance is the concept of group unity, achieved by placing individual personalities and actions secondary to group functioning. A newcomer may have the need to unburden himself or herself to others. But prolonged airing of personal grievances is unlikely to lead to a beneficial interchange of ideas, which is an understood purpose of the meeting. Every member has experience, strength and hope to be shared. Meetings are made up of talking and listening. Both are essential, but an extreme of either one can deprive others of help. Those with experience and those who are new and eager to learn can both grow spiritually by sharing openly with one another at a meeting.

No one group member has authority over other members. For this reason, group officers are changed as often as possible. When a member has been elected to a specific office, it is looked upon as an opportunity to serve others and not as a means to direct or control group activities. It is important that a spirit of equality is maintained in the Al-Anon group. So that no member comes to feel overly important or even indispensable in some capacity, the group changes its leadership regularly.

Important decisions are made by the group as a whole, by appealing to the group conscience. Members are reminded through the Traditions that the source of spiritual strength—"a loving God as He may express Himself"—speaks through different members at different times. There is a comfortable feeling in knowing that guidance for the group comes not through individuals, but from the willingness of the group to follow whatever wisdom may be expressed through the membership in the course of the meeting.

The Al-Anon program is unique in that it is a spiritually based, non-professional, non-profit self-help organization. It is designed for and led by the relatives and friends of alcoholics. Members meet together for mutual aid. Al-Anon is not affiliated with the growing number of professional programs or treatment centers for family members which are run on different lines with different objectives. Al-Anon is aware of the many pressures and influences that may serve to dilute the Al-Anon program. Often members may be involved in other causes, therapies, religions, philosophies or organizations. Thoughts that do not reflect the Al-Anon point of view may be introduced into meeting discussions by chance. Often, by adhering closely to the Twelve Steps and Twelve Traditions, such thinking can be discerned and dealt with according to the conscience of the group.

Another source of confusion is that members may also be affected by additions other than alcohol, such as drug dependence, gambling or compulsive eating. There are other programs for these family members and friends. Al-Anon's only requirement for membership is that there is a problem of alcoholism in a relative or a friend. Individual Al-Anon members may choose other organizations from which to seek help for other problems. Because Al-Anon does not oppose or endorse these other programs, the Traditions ensure that the distinctive character and purpose of the Al-Anon groups is preserved.

Al-Anon is well aware that in these times of public awareness of the disease of alcoholism, problems of money, property and prestige can divert family members from the primary spiritual aim of the program: to help families of alcoholics. For this reason, Al-Anon groups are financially self-supporting and also make contributions to the maintenance of Al-Anon's service centers. Financed solely by the Al-Anon membership, these service centers and committees are directly responsible to those they serve. In this way the name of Al-Anon remains apart from public, or controversial, issues.

An uncommon aspect of the Al-Anon program is the carefully guarded anonymity of individual members, both in Al-Anon and A.A. The foundation of Al-Anon's public relations policy is attraction rather than promotion, although the availability of help for suffering family members is sometimes shared through the media. Personal anonymity at this level is preserved in accordance with the spiritual principles.

Most remarkable about these Twelve Traditions of the Al-Anon Program is that they work. Groups that adhere closely to this set of guidelines grow and flourish. Others may become diverted or diluted by problems arising from confused ideas about what the Al-Anon program is, and what it is not. Fortunately, a ready willingness to seek guidance through the Traditions often puts the group back on track again, so that it can continue to focus on the common welfare of its members and help others.

OTHER TOOLS OF THE PROGRAM

The Slogans

The Al-Anon program embraces a set of principles that are at once simple and profound. A newcomer who enters the Al-Anon/Alateen meeting room in confusion and deep pain about the drinking cannot grasp a complicated philosophy. Such a person is desperate for relief from suffering. Beyond the warmth, caring and understanding offered by other members are a handful of simple phrases they will share with the newcomer, known as the "slogans." These are often the first tools the despairing person is able to hear and hold onto; but they are more than the commonplace, well-worn phrases that they first appear to be. The slogans have opened many a closed mind and have given suffering family members the first ray of hope that life can be different.

Once an individual has experienced this capacity for change, a slogan accepted at first for its simplicity takes on deeper and deeper meaning. Understanding of the principles progresses with recovery.

Easy Does It

No one has ever suggested that living with all the complexities resulting from alcoholism is an easy undertaking! Why, then, the slogan *Easy Does It?* Because alcoholism has affected the family's well-being in so many ways. There are or have been at one time or another money problems, health problems, work problems, problems with the children in school, at home or with friends. Most families suffer the deep fear and anxiety that somebody outside the family will find out about or condemn them for all the problems.

Many who are deeply affected by someone else's drinking have spent sleepless nights wondering how to get all the problems solved, with one thought chasing another in an endless round of helplessness and frustration. All too often, a resolve to tackle a single problem gets side-tracked by a new crisis the next day or the next week, and then the same whirling thoughts, or even panic reactions, begin all over again.

When Al-Anon/Alateen members refer to *Easy Does It,* they are not suggesting *more* action, they are suggesting *less* action, less frantic involvement with the behavior of others and, therefore, less frustration. In other words, they are free to set the pace of living that suits them, not anybody else, including the alcoholic. Now they are able to participate in activities with others that will provide meaning and comfort, instead of constantly repeating old patterns of behavior.

Members can learn to make the best possible use of their time and energy, to "roll with the punches" and to really choose how to tackle problems one at a time. Further, they may make decisions in the manner they think best and at a time when they are ready for it. Once they have grasped the principle of this great tension-relaxer, they can begin to apply it elsewhere in life. Normal involvement with the problems of others can be separated from abnormal involvement. *Easy Does It* is the key to that difference.

For those who are no longer affected by the problems engendered by active alcoholism, this everyday phrase can lead to increased peace of mind. At first it may appear meaningless—until the individual searches out the tremendous significance hidden within it. Not only does *Easy Does It* break the cycle of tension and anxiety, but it releases the person from irritations that are a part of daily living. It is a beautiful, practical tool for smoothing out confused thinking and impatient, headlong words and actions. It is a resource with lifelong usefulness.

Let Go And Let God

Although they may express it in different ways, everyone seems to feel a great sense of responsibility toward the effects of alcoholism. One will make good the alcoholic's promises to pay; another will cover up someone else's absences from work; a third may take the drinker to task by trying to "straighten him out" in one way or another. When this fails, the family member, supervisor or close friend feels very much alone and somehow responsible for the failure. This may lead to a redoubling of their efforts to obtain results, accompanied by the same sense of failure and the same feeling that they are somehow to blame.

Al-Anon suggests that there are other sources of well-being for the alcoholic; such a provider may be God, in Al-Anon often called the Higher Power. Thus, the individual is not alone and not solely responsible for the effects of this disease. *Let Go And Let God* indicates that this principle is really an exercise in humility. Family members and friends do not have the power to change alcoholic behavior. No one can control the actions of others, alcoholic or not.

If friends and relatives will let go of their own often misguided desire to help and allow a spiritual source to guide the alcoholic instead, surprising results often follow. At Al-Anon meetings, members will proudly share how they have refrained from making excuses, or covering up the consequences of the drinking, only to find that the alcoholic has taken on some responsibility for himself or herself by paying bills or getting to work. Even if *Let Go and Let God* results in the alcoholic's getting into more trouble—with the law, for instance, or with the boss—the person deeply affected by the drinking comes to realize that he or she is not responsible.

Also, by maintaining a healthy detachment from the consequences of the alcoholic behavior, others may be in a better position to act and think clearly in situations that require personal responsibility.

At this deeper level, members learn to appreciate that they have little or no control over the affairs of others and can only be responsible for themselves. Practice of *Let Go And Let God* leads to a profound realization of how frequently a Higher Power does intervene in the lives of others and how wise the solutions presented are. Most, but not all, Al-Anon members actively seek guidance from this spiritual source for the direction of their own lives and for the lives of others, believing that it is superior to all the efforts of the human intellect and the human will. Such a person is able to maintain a sense of well-being in the face of many difficulties whether alcoholic in nature or not.

First Things First

Many a distressed person comes to Al-Anon believing that once the alcoholic stops drinking, all the problems will disappear. What a disappointment to find out this is not so! What is more, alcoholism has been so much the center of focus that other aspects of living have been neglected. Many spouses have become so obsessed with the drinking that they have failed to monitor their own health or perhaps their own compulsive behavior, have not carried through their intentions to continue their own education or take that promised vacation. A young alcoholic may have absorbed so much of his or her parents' attention that brothers and sisters have been short-changed. The professional may have let other aspects of his or her work slip, or have neglected other employees.

First Things First allows everyone to take exclusive attention off the alcoholic problem and begin to assess the relative importance of all aspects of living. In admitting that responses to the alcoholic behavior are usually out of proportion to the situation, this clarification of the order of importance clears the way for more constructive living.

When members begin to focus on themselves, according to the principle of *First Things First,* the self-knowledge that results places them in a better position to proceed to a life of order. If the decision is made to solve a single problem, the success achieved results in a feeling of well-being. The spouse may decide to get a long overdue medical check-up. A husband of an alcoholic wife may decide that his children need the care of a neighbor or a housekeeper while he is at work. A parent may decide that his alcoholic youngster may no longer be permitted to drive the family car. *First Things First* permits the individual to progress steadily toward recovery by choosing the next step.

If sobriety for the alcoholic does come, *First Things First* still ensures that the family member or friend continues a life of serenity in the face of profound change. Rather than wondering how many A.A. meetings the alcoholic is attending or whether he or she will drink again, Al-Anon/Alateen members focus on their own recovery by continuing to seek lives of calmness and order.

First Things First, in a spiritual sense, leads to an understanding that each person should concentrate on his or her own spiritual and emotional health in order to maintain a sense of contentment with life, rather than depending upon the actions of others, alcoholic or not.

Live And Let Live

The slogan *Live And Let Live* speaks profoundly of relationships with alcoholics and with others.

Al-Anon and Alateen members are challenged to live a full life, despite the circumstances. They are encouraged to put aside all personal feelings of guilt, failure and recrimination and to find life enjoyable. In seeking a fuller life, many will reach out to one another by telephone to share in their search for a life of serenity and happiness through simple and obtainable things—the enjoyment of good weather, a sunset, a chat with a neighbor or co-worker, a chance to be of service to someone else. They have learned the trick that problems seem to diminish in direct correlation to one's ability to put them in their true perspective. Others are blessed with a sense of humor that enables them to keep a sense of proportion about themselves and their circumstances.

The second part of the slogan, "Let Live," allows Al-Anon members not to judge the behavior of others, including the alcoholic. Few people always act in a way that can withstand close scrutiny by others, and judgment is reserved for the authority invested in a Higher Power. Those who accept the slogan *Live And*

Let Live come to understand that tolerance adds to the quality of daily living, whereas resentment and self-pity diminish the human capacity to live joyfully.

Frequently, all that is needed to lead a more rewarding life is a change in attitude, rather than a change in circumstances.

Each of these slogans represents a particular spiritual discipline. They provide a logical starting point for dealing with many situations. They are also easy to recall in times of stress. An individual's response to them can be used as a measuring stick in evaluating his or her progress along the road to personal recovery.

The Serenity Prayer

> *God grant me the serenity*
> *To accept the things I cannot change,*
> *Courage to change the things I can,*
> *And wisdom to know the difference.*

This prayer is often said at the beginning or ending of Al-Anon meetings. It is also used as a daily reminder by many Al-Anon members in times of quiet meditation, or as a guide in moments of stress. Like so much of the Al-Anon program, it combines comfort, inspiration and practicability.

The three key concepts in the Serenity Prayer are acceptance, courage and wisdom. Al-Anon members aspire to these qualities in their search for recovery and growing emotional maturity. The simple repetition of this prayer means that each Al-Anon member continues to take a glance down the road to recovery to make sure that his or her daily path leads toward this goal.

To many Al-Anon newcomers, the idea of accepting the disease of alcoholism is not an easy one. Acceptance of all that is distressing seems like a sign of weakness. It can be argued that if a person is an upright, intelligent, strong or loving person, then he or she has the necessary qualities to force a change in the alcoholic situation. Before Al-Anon, many a struggling individual has tried desperately to change others by attempting to live up to standards that are close to perfection. Put another way, newcomers may think they can remake the alcoholic so that he or she conforms to what is expected of a spouse, parent, child, friend, employee and so on. Many newcomers enter the Al-Anon program feeling quite worn out by the struggle to get others, especially the alcoholic, to toe the line and do what is expected of them.

To accept that they do not have the power to make the alcoholic stop drinking is the first order of business for newcomers. This surrender to the inevitable comes quickly to people whose perceptions have been blunted by living with so much pain for so long. Often, the acceptance that someone close to them has a serious, complex disease over which neither the sick person nor anyone else has any control, is arrived at only after much soul-searching and sharing with other Al-Anon members. But once acceptance of the reality of alcoholism comes about and resistance to the nature of the disease is at an end, the road to recovery is made clear at last.

Sooner or later the Al-Anon member is confronted with a choice. Having acquired an understanding of alcoholism and how this disease affects others, what should be done about it? One the one hand, it is quite possible to walk away from a situation that seems unendurable. On the other hand, the Al-Anon member is surrounded by others who have come to terms with similar circumstances in a variety of ways.

Al-Anon, through its suggestions, encourages the search for personal solutions within the framework of the entire Al-Anon program. It asks of the newcomer not to be too hasty in reaching a conclusion before considering all the alternatives. Courage is needed to take a long, honest look at how he or she has contributed to the situation. It is not easy for the newcomer to admit that his or her own behavior has at times been irrational. It takes courage to extract the negative personal qualities buried beneath the confusion of alcoholism masking their presence, and more courage to be willing to change them. Al-Anon members do this without making excuses for their own behavior, or without indulging the human tendency to blame others. In this way, Al-Anon members develop a realistic concept of what they are able to change in the situation, whether the alcoholic continues to drink or not.

With a growing sense that much can be done to improve the situation, the Al-Anon member can make a reappraisal of the alcoholic dilemma. With a quiet mind, unhampered by resentment and bitterness, he or she is free to make decisions in their own best interests and of others who are close to them. The wisdom to choose rightly is sought from the guidance of a spiritual source—the Al-Anon group, a Higher Power, or the God of that member's understanding. In seeking the right answer, the Al-Anon member experiences a lessening of reliance on self-will and an increase in discernment between what can realistically be achieved and what cannot. Frequently, relinquishing that which cannot be changed is experienced as relief, an unburdening, or peace of mind. Al-Anon members describe it as serenity.

A change in thinking and feeling leads to a change in attitude toward the situation. Acceptance becomes a source of strength and freedom, and changing "the things I can" becomes a lifetime program. A deeper understanding of what it means to be human leads inevitably toward a source of wisdom and power outside oneself. Al-Anon members come to realize that they have found a sound philosophy for living that reaches far beyond the immediate situation.

*Sponsorship

The framework for recovery, as described so far, has outlined the changes in attitude needed for growth in the Al-Anon program. In other words, Al-Anon and Alateen members learn to stop focusing on the alcoholic or others by looking realistically at themselves and thus are able to make changes in their own lives.

So often the complex details of problems make them appear to be insoluble. What should be done about the finances? How should the wife or parent respond to a call from the police? Should a distracted husband or father take his employer, his doctor, or his child's teacher into his confidence? What can be done about violence or sexual abuse? While the Al-Anon member is free to discuss such pressing questions at an Al-Anon meeting, some are so complex that they may require the attention of well-schooled professionals. Then, too, there is seldom that much time for the group to devote to the needs of any one of its members. While personal problems can be shared at beginners meetings, all newcomers are encouraged to acquire an Al-Anon sponsor.

The name "sponsor" is given to the Al-Anon member selected by the newcomer to act as a personal guide and friend. Usually, the person chosen is of the same sex, has had a similar involvement with alcoholism and is recovered sufficiently in the Al-Anon program to share encouragement and experience using

*See also (#P-31) Sponsorship, What It's all About

Al-Anon's tools of recovery. As Al-Anon members, sponsors do not give advice. They share their own experiences, which may or may not have been of a similar nature. Sponsorship is an informal relationship that may be terminated by either person at any time. But frequently both find they develop a close friendship which broadens beyond the problems that first united them.

A sponsor can be the emotional lifeline that the newcomer needs. Many people come into the Al-Anon program lonely and resentful. The sponsor is the person who will listen to the newcomer with patience and empathy. This is most frequently done by telephone between Al-Anon meetings. Just putting the problem into words helps to make everything clearer. Very slowly, a good sponsor will make suggestions, one idea at a time, that will lead the newcomer toward more constructive channels of thinking. Most importantly, a sponsor will introduce the concept of detachment from alcoholism by pointing out the futility of pouring out liquor, hiding it, or meddling and scheming to prevent the drinking. A hands-off policy is needed to redirect the family member's energies toward more constructive activities. This same concept of focusing on oneself is a necessary tool in maintaining harmony long after active alcoholism ceases to be a part of family life. Sponsors of those who no longer live with active alcoholics are quick to point out that personal recovery continues whether or not the alcoholic stops drinking.

Consistent with the principles of Al-Anon, a good sponsor does not give advice, nor act as a spokesman for the Al-Anon program. This is especially important in the area of major family problems, such as whether or not to go to court, to seek professional assistance, separation or divorce. The role of a sponsor is to be a sounding board, comforter and builder-up of an often battered personality. In this way the person sponsored can adopt the right frame of mind to make important decisions for themselves. Talking to a sponsor may discourage rash action at the beginning of the Al-Anon program. Nor does the sponsor become involved personally in the problem itself. A sponsor also discourages emotional dependency. A good sponsor stresses the wisdom of considering *all* suggestions offered by the Al-Anon program.

Yet, knowing that people learn from each other, a sponsor will share his or her own experiences with the person sponsored. The fundamental points the sponsor will gently get across are that problems become soluble when they are divided into pieces of manageable size. A newcomer learns that he or she can accept any problem for just one day, or one hour if need be. Dwelling on the past is futile; re-hashing past grievances only makes them hurt all over again. Projecting into the future, or trying to imagine what is going to happen, is also useless. Dread of what might happen, or trying to outguess the alcoholic, is a self-defeating occupation.

A good sponsor encourages the use of all the Al-Anon tools, such as the Serenity Prayer, the slogans and the Twelve Steps of Recovery. As time progresses, a sponsor will encourage the newcomer to lean more and more upon the help offered through the Al-Anon meetings, whether by attending beginners' meetings, reading the Al-Anon Conference-Approved Literature, or becoming active in an Al-Anon group by taking on one of the volunteer positions that help a group to function effectively.

Giving a large amount of emotional support to the newcomer is the sponsor's contribution. But a sponsor benefits in return. The trust and confidence that grows between sponsor and sponsored is a form of communication that supports and nourishes. Sometimes the newcomer learns for the first time what it is to have a deep and meaningful relationship with another person.

Conference-Approved Literature

An important additional tool for learning about the family disease of alcoholism, and for studying Al-Anon's principles in depth, is the Al-Anon/Alateen literature. This book is an example. New Al-Anon/Alateen literature begins with the approval of the World Service Conference and is written anonymously by Al-Anon and Alateen members. The final editing is done by long-time members, or professional writers who are also members. Manuscripts are submitted to an Al-Anon Literature Committee which acts for the fellowship. They are also read by the Al-Anon General Secretary and members of the Policy Committee before publication.

Al-Anon is aware that there is a growing number of publications from other sources on the family disease of alcoholism. To keep Al-Anon's message unified and in focus, it is suggested that only Conference-Approved Literature be used and distributed at Al-Anon meetings, conferences and conventions. The literature is also used to inform professionals, outside agencies and individuals about the Al-Anon/Alateen groups and their availability as resources in the community.

Members are encouraged to help themselves to the readily available supply of literature at any Al-Anon/Alateen meeting. Usually the pamphlets are free of charge to the individual member and have been purchased by the group for the express purpose of sharing the Al-Anon program.

There are a number of pamphlets on every conceivable aspect of the family involvement in the disease of alcoholism, written with insight and sensitivity by other Al-Anon members. There are also booklets on related topics, such as LIVING WITH SO-

BRIETY and BLUEPRINT FOR PROGRESS: AL-ANON'S FOURTH STEP INVENTORY. A much-loved and much-used small hardcover book is ONE DAY AT A TIME IN AL-ANON (sometimes abbreviated to ODAT). A parallel book for Alateens is ALATEEN—*a day at a time.* These books provide a short reading and reminder for each day of the year. Many members rely on these tools to keep their focus on the positive aspects of daily living.

Among the other hardcover books for which a moderate charge is generally made is a basic book, AL-ANON FAMILY GROUPS (formerly titled LIVING WITH AN ALCOHOLIC). LOIS REMEMBERS is a history of the founding of Al-Anon by one of its much-loved co-founders, Lois W. An extensive analysis of Al-Anon's TWELVE STEPS AND TWELVE TRADITIONS is found in the book of that name. The basic concepts of Alateen are found in the hardcover ALATEEN: HOPE FOR CHILDREN OF ALCOHOLICS, and the difficulties of alcoholism in the family are expressed in THE DILEMMA OF THE ALCOHOLIC MARRIAGE. This book, AL-ANON FACES ALCOHOLISM, was designed to provide a multifaceted approach for everyone interested in the effects of the disease on others.

Also available at many Al-Anon meetings and by subscription are copies of Al-Anon/Alateen's monthly magazine, The FORUM, which is reviewed by a committee and the WSO staff, assuring that the publication represents understanding and growth in the Al-Anon program. The FORUM also offers meeting ideas and materials for group discussions. Subscriptions are available to individuals and groups. In addition there are many service newsletters which keep groups aware of current activities and new program aids.

Al-Anon/Alateen Conference-Approved Literature has been translated into many other languages. Although local customs and culture may vary, the spirit and meaning of Al-Anon's principles of recovery are being spread through the literature to an ever-widening circle of people throughout the world.

AL-ANON: A WORLDWIDE FRIENDSHIP

The human needs and spiritual ideas of Al-Anon know no national boundaries. "Al-Anon is a worldwide friendship," writes a member after visiting groups in many other countries. For wherever alcoholic drinking has brought confusion and despair, Al-Anon can offer comfort, hope and understanding.

Groups are flourishing on the North American continent, both in the United States and Canada, and in Central and South America. Al-Anon is well represented in the English-speaking countries of Europe, South Africa, Australia and New Zealand. Nor have language differences deterred the establishment of groups throughout Europe, India and Japan. Members in other countries have received permission to translate the Al-Anon literature into 17 of their own languages for distribution to others who need help.

From 1951, when Al-Anon began, until 1961, when the Al-Anon World Service Conference was initiated, the link between the growing number of Al-Anon groups was maintained by a number of dedicated volunteers and a few paid workers in the New York Clearing House. In 1954 several members of this Clearing House committee were the incorporators of a non-profit membership corporation, which was named Al-Anon Family Group Headquarters, Inc. Because of its nature, the headquarters became known as the World Service Office (WSO). A

Board of Directors with the help of an Advisory Board settled matters of policy.

Communication by mail with the WSO was effective in the early days of the Al-Anon fellowship. As Al-Anon grew, it was decided that the voice of the membership should be heard by a more direct means. Looking to the future, it was feared that the WSO could become remote from the groups it served and risk losing touch with the concerns of Al-Anon as a whole.

Al-Anon followed the path of A.A. By 1961, Al-Anon agreed that the group conscience of the fellowship as a whole could best be heard through a Conference of Delegates from all sections of the United States and Canada. The Conference was to meet yearly with the Board of Trustees and the World Service Office administrative staff. The first Conference was initiated in 1961 on a trial basis. By 1963, the linkage between the groups and the World Service Office proved to be so effective that its members voted unanimously to make the arrangement permanent. A Conference Charter was adopted in 1967. It is a traditional, not a legal, framework within which the Conference functions. In the meantime, the name "Board of Directors" was changed to Board of Trustees, (and the Conference supplanted the original Advisory Board). An Executive Committee was established to aid in the conduct of administrative affairs.

Since the days of this pioneering work to meet the needs of the Al-Anon fellowship as a whole, Al-Anon groups in other countries have established their own Conferences. Members in these countries now elect Delegates to a general services meeting designed to seek the best way to carry the Al-Anon message of recovery to families and friends of alcoholics amid cultural and language differences. Also, representatives from these General Service Conferences have been invited to attend the World Service Conference with voice, but without a vote. All who love the Al-Anon program welcome the shaping of Al-Anon's concepts of service to meet the needs of the fellowship as it continues to grow throughout the world.

HOW TO FIND HELP

If you have read through this book, or even a few pages, and said to yourself: "I feel like that" or "I have felt like that" or "This is talking about *my* experience," then Al-Anon or Alateen can be for you. If this book has made you feel just slightly uncomfortable, if you are or ever have been bothered by the drinking of someone close to you, then Al-Anon or Alateen may be for you. These groups stand ready to share the Program of Recovery with you, if you want it—but you must want it. Accept the fact that change must begin with you.

If you are willing to change your point of view about the disease of alcoholism and the way it affects those involved, then help is readily available.

It is as near as your telephone. Look up the Al-Anon number in your telephone book and speak to an Al-Anon or Alateen member who understands, who knows what you are talking about. There is no need to give your name. You may keep your anonymity—that is all part of the Al-Anon program. There are 25,000 Al-Anon and Alateen Family Groups worldwide. But if there is no telephone listing, or if you are remote from an Al-Anon meeting, then write:

Al-Anon Family Group Headquarters, Inc.
Box 862, Midtown Station
New York, N.Y. 10018-0862

You will receive a reply from a understanding Al-Anon member. There are also a number of "loners" in the Al-Anon program who keep in touch by mail.

A call to Al-Anon will provide you with information on where and when the Al-Anon groups nearest you hold their meetings. You will probably be referred to a contact person who will welcome you and help you get started with the group. Devote some time to reading about alcoholism. It will give you a new view of your problem and help you deal with it more effectively. A call to the nearest A.A. Intergroup will give you information about open A.A. meetings where anyone is welcome and you can hear alcoholics talk about their recovery.

If you are a professional and are interested to know how Al-Anon can assist your client or your patient, please contact Al-Anon by phone or by letter. Staff members from Al-Anon Intergroup Offices or Al-Anon Family Group Headquarters are very willing to share information with you. Al-Anon literature, much of it in the form of single-sheet, easy-to-read pamphlets, can be obtained upon request.

Index

Index